SHUT UP
AND
SELL MORE

Weddings & Events

Disc Jockey Edition

*Ask better questions,
listen to the answers
and grow your business*

by **ALAN BERG, CSP**

Left of Center Marketing & Publishing
Ideas for when business isn't right

This book is dedicated to my family,

who put up with my frequent

traveling and seemingly unending

attention to my work.

Carole, Adam & Ian,

I love you and couldn't do this

without your love and support.

Shut Up and Sell More Weddings & Events
Disc Jockey Edition
Australia Paperback ISBN: 978-0-9889179-8-9

Published by
Left of Center Marketing & Publishing
Kendall Park, NJ © 2020
No part of this book may be used in any manner without written permission. For more information, contact Alan Berg at SellMore@AlanBerg.com

Acknowledgements:
I would like to thank the following for their contributions to this book:
Editors: Carole Berg, Adam J. Berg & Katie Lee
Book Design: Ian T. Berg & Alan Berg
Cover Design: Ian T. Berg

Written and Printed in the USA

Thanks to my sales manager, and mentor, at a Chrysler dealership, Al "Cee" Chiudina, for telling me to "shut up", which helped steer my sales career upward. The lessons he taught me continue to pay dividends year after year, as I hope they will for you.

TABLE OF CONTENTS

	Preface - the story behind the title	9
	Introduction – A career in sales	13
1	It all starts with a sale	19
2	Ask better questions	23
3	Yes or No vs. open-ended questions	27
4	Understanding your brand	33
5	Invest in your success	37
6	The 4 steps to more sales	41
7	Marketing is like a relay race	47
8	Getting more inquiries	51
9	How many buying signals have happened by the time you get an inquiry?	57
10	Creating better calls-to-action	61
11	Why do they always ask "How much…?"	67
12	4 ways to handle pricing questions and pricing on your website	71
13	What are you really selling?	77
14	Getting more appointments	85
15	Do you want to be happy or right?	91
16	Having better appointments	95

17	Hit the reset button	101
18	Your marketing materials won't close the sale for you	107
19	Make it all about them, and assume the sale	111
20	Don't have a sales pitch, just talk to them	115
21	Asking better questions	119
22	Help them buy	125
23	Objections overruled!	129
24	Handling specific objections	135
25	Asking for the sale	141
26	When to ask for the sale	149
27	Discounting versus Negotiating	153
28	What's your opportunity cost?	159
29	Packages vs. a-la-carte	163
30	The power of 3's	171
31	Top down selling for a better bottom line	175
32	Follow up to increase your profits	183
33	You can't do their wedding or event, if you don't close the sale	187
	From the author	190
	About the author	192

PREFACE

The Story Behind The Title

> **Author's note:** This special edition of Shut Up and Sell More Weddings & Events is for Disc Jockeys (DJs), entertainment, lighting and photo booth companies. If you've already read the original edition, most of this is going to be the same for you. I've updated and changed the references to be specifically applicable to wedding and event DJs. It will certainly be a good refresher for you, I just want to be transparent. If you've not read the original book, this will be all new to you. Thanks for choosing this book, and I look forward to your feedback and seeing how else I can help you succeed.

I didn't set out to be in sales, it just happened. As a matter of fact it's happened to most of you reading this as well. If you work for, or own a company you're part of the sales process. Every link in the supply chain feeds the sales process. If you make something, that goes into something, that someone buys, or you do a service that someone pays for, or you interact with a customer in any way, you're part of the sales process. That's true whether you intended to be in sales or not. I've wanted to write a book about sales for a while. I've been either doing sales personally, managing a team of salespeople, training salespeople, or speaking about sales for most of my adult life. The skills I've learned, and honed, have served me well, and I've helped many people, just like you, sell more, and feel better about the process.

This book will share with you what I've learned along the way. Most of mine was on-the-job training, not book or classroom training. I started out, as a teenager, selling my rock and roll band. I managed a retail store, and then I had a small burglar alarm business. Each of these gave me different skills, but it wasn't until I started selling cars that I got my deep training. I didn't have a grand plan to sell cars. A good friend's father bought a Chrysler dealership and a year later I got a call asking if I wanted to sell for them.

Customer satisfaction has always been my focus. Sure, I wanted to make the sale, but I also wanted a happy customer. After all, happy customers come back and buy again, and send you their friends. Product knowledge is, and will always be, an important part of the sales process. Long before I started selling cars, I accompanied my friend while buying his first new car. When I asked the salesman if the car was front wheel drive, or rear wheel drive (which shouldn't be a difficult question for him), he didn't know. I was shocked that he didn't know the answer to such a basic and important question. When I started selling cars I vowed never to be like that guy. So I always made it a point to study the new product books every model year.

A year after I started with the dealership, Chrysler decided that their salespeople should be more knowledgeable about the cars. That way we would stand out when customers went shopping around and they'd come back to us. To motivate their salespeople, they created a product information contest called the "Auto Know Competition", because you "ought-to-know". In the car business, as with most, nothing motivates competitive sales teams quite like money and prizes. The very first year they had the competition I was the national champion. That's right, out of all of the Chrysler salespeople in the country, I was the winner. The finals were in the form of a game show, in a TV studio in Detroit. I even got one of those oversize checks, for $5,000 (like the ones you see at the end of a golf tournament).

Needless to say, when I got back to my dealership I was feeling pretty good about myself. One day my sales manager, Al Cee, put his arm around me and said *"Alan, you know more about these cars than anyone I've ever met, in 20 years in this business."* I told him *"Thanks"*, and then he said *"Good, now Shut Up!"* I was confused. He had just told me I know more than anyone he'd ever met, but he wanted me to shut up? He went on to tell me that he had been shadowing me with my customers (staying within earshot and listening to the conversation) and I had been telling them things they hadn't asked about.

I didn't think it was true but he recounted specific things I had said, without the customers asking. You may be wondering, what's wrong with that? I was too. What I realized is that when we offer up information that customers don't ask about, we run the risk of bringing up things that they either don't care about, or worse, that have a negative effect on the sales process. That's called selling yourself right out of the sale. What I was to learn is that, given the opportunity, customers will tell you everything you need to know to make the sale. You just have to give them the chance. I didn't realize how hard it was going to be to break me of my talking too much habit, or how rewarding it would be, once I did.

When I took to heart his advice to Shut Up, I went from being a pretty good salesperson, to a top salesperson. I was number 1 or 2 in sales in our dealership most months. I went on to win the Auto Know national championship 4 years in a row. In my last year selling cars I was also in the Top 50 Club, which meant I was one of the top 50 Chrysler salespeople in the country by volume. To qualify we also had to have a customer satisfaction rating of 90% or higher. So you see, you can have high volume and satisfied customers.

So, thank you for picking up this book. You've taken an important step towards making more sales, and having both you, and your customers feel better about the process.

INTRODUCTION

A Career In Sales

The informal sales training I had received laid the groundwork for my next sales career, selling wedding advertising. While I had heard the expressions *"sales is sales"* and *"it doesn't matter what you sell as long as you believe in it"*, car sales and wedding magazine sales couldn't have been more different. Car sales is showroom sales, an inside sales position. We, the salespeople, waited around for customers to come in. It was the dealership's job to get us the foot traffic. Once they came in, it was our job to make the sale.

When I was selling wedding advertising it was outside sales. It was also cold-calling (going to businesses who had not expressed an interest in our product - magazine advertising - and phoning or walking in to try to make a sale). I would get in my car, every day, and drive around, walking in to businesses around my territory, which was New Jersey and the Hudson Valley in New York (the counties just above New York City).

My car sales job had come with perks - a company car,

base salary, health insurance, and even lunch on Saturdays (they didn't want us to leave on the busiest day of the week). By contrast, for my advertising sales job I was an independent contractor, not an employee. I had no salary, no draw against future commissions, no guarantee or base pay, no benefits, and I was on straight commission. If I sold, I got paid. If I didn't sell, I got nothing. I paid my own gas, tolls, expenses, internet connection and phone. Heck, I even paid for the computer, printer, paper, toner and fax machine. Since I had given back my company car, I had to go and buy a car. Oh, and I forgot to mention that when I took that job I was married, we had a 3-year old son and my wife was pregnant. No pressure to produce, right?

So why did I take the job? On paper it seemed wrong. I had left Chrysler to become the leasing manager at a Honda dealership. Only instead of being the leasing manager, which was the job I had wanted, I was made the Business Manager (who also handled the leasing). That's the person you see after you buy your car, whose job it is to sell you all those other things you don't want (extended warranties, alarm systems, body side moldings, and more).

I just didn't feel comfortable in that position. I had previously learned to really listen to customers and sell them what they wanted. Now, here I was in a position where my job was to sell them things they didn't want. I felt a strong lack of integrity. Worse than that, I was never home with my wife or young son. When I gave them 2-weeks' notice that I was leaving, all they could do was show me how much money I was making. Despite hating the job, I did it well. My father always taught me that if you take a job, do it to the best of your ability. If you don't like the job, don't do it poorly, just leave. So, while I was there I did it well, better than they had hoped. But when they told me how much money I was on track to be earning all I could say was *"It's not the money!"* And when I uttered those words I had a feeling of relief come over me, because I really meant it.

I didn't understand that before, I thought it was always about the money. After all, as salespeople that's how we are judged, by our sales. But the money doesn't make the job better. The money doesn't make up for not being home. The money really doesn't make you happy. So when my friend called and asked if I wanted a commission-only, independent contractor sales job, driving around unfamiliar areas, selling a product I didn't yet know, to people who hadn't asked me to come, I jumped at the chance. That jump was a leap of faith, but one tempered by the confidence that I knew how to sell, and sell well.

Selling advertising for WeddingPages magazine started out as mostly outside sales, meeting face-to-face with my customers. Then it became a lot of phone sales, and later email became the focus. After a few years, my wife and I purchased the two magazine franchises for which I'd been selling. That led to me publishing those two WeddingPages magazines, which also meant leading a team of salespeople and a production team. This was our business, not someone else's. After 5 years we sold our magazine franchises back to the franchisor. They had asked me to become a regional sales director, managing a team of salespeople from Boston down to Washington DC. Shortly after taking that position WeddingPages was bought by The Knot (at the time a 3-year old startup wedding website, that had just gone public with their initial public stock offering - IPO). The Knot was, at the time, the leading wedding website.

After a few years I was promoted to Vice President of Local Sales, leading a team of 50 to 60 sales people around the country to sell tens of millions of dollars in advertising, each year. Over 11 years I held various positions at The Knot, many of which included hiring and training our local sales reps. Much of the sales training program was created under my direction. I also created the Local Client Relations Managers team, which was a new way of doing customer service. It was very customer-centric and a big change from the way it was done there before.

Along the way I had been on stage, speaking about sales and business at conferences, large and small, local and national.

My aim is to help wedding & event DJs, just like you, make more sales. And now, more than 25 years after falling into the wedding & event industry, in addition to consulting and speaking for WeddingPro, the education arm of The Knot Worldwide (the leading wedding media company with websites in 18 countries), I find myself traveling the world, speaking about sales, business and success.

If making sales is a key part of your job, you can do it better. Whether you've been in DJ sales for 20 years, or 20 minutes, there are tips and ideas in this book that will help you. It truly was when I learned to stop talking, and listen better, that I started to sell more. That's a skill that continues to bring me success. I know it will help you as well. How can I be so sure? These are the same tips that I've been teaching and speaking about at conferences, and in the private sales training I do for entertinament companies, like yours. The feedback I've gotten is how I can be sure. People with 20 years of sales experience tell me that they appreciate being reminded of the basics, and that they've picked up some new ideas. People who are new to sales tell me that they now feel more comfortable doing sales, and that they're selling more. It's been a crazy, wild ride, and it's far from over. So, thanks for picking up this book and please share your successes with me.

CHAPTER 1

It all starts with a sale

The difference between a hobby and a business is sales. Sales turns an artist into an entrepreneur; an idea into an empire. No matter how talented you are, how creative you are or how skilled you are, you don't have a business until you make a sale. Sales is not a dirty word, it's an exciting one, because it shows that people value what you do for them.

Anyone who comes into contact with a customer or potential customer is in sales. That interaction can make or break the relationship. Whether you're the owner of a DJ company, an event planner, a janitor, a receptionist or delivery driver, if you have contact with customers, you're in sales. How you interact with your customers affects how they perceive your business, which in turn affects your sales.

Unfortunately, what makes you so good at your skill or trade probably doesn't qualify you to be in sales. Right-brained, creative types, don't necessarily make the best salespeople. Creative artists often have trouble with the sales process because they're too close to their work. How do you place a value on a piece of art? How do you place a value on a your MC style, the way you mix songs or the way you produce and event?

How to specifically price your products and services is a topic for another book, or a consultation, but I will touch on pricing a little later, including how to handle that pesky *"How much do you charge?"* question. You don't get to do what you love to do, until you make a sale. Actually that's not correct. You can do that same skill without getting paid, but that's called volunteering or a hobby. It becomes a business when someone gives you something of value in return. Bartering was the original currency, but these days we trade our services and products for money, in some form: cash, credit, check, bitcoin. While many businesses still include barter transactions, trading service/product for service/product, that doesn't pay the bills.

The sale starts the wheels of your business in motion, culminating with getting to deliver your product or service to the customer. That product or service is probably the reason you opened your business in the first place. It was the passion for music, lighting, production, weddings, etc., combined with the skill to deliver those products or services at a high enough level that others would want to give you value for it. Doing your skill at a high level is not enough to be in business. You have to learn to be good at business as well. With each of the businesses I've owned or managed came new opportunities to learn how to be better at business.

Every sale you make teaches you how to be better the next time. Every sale you lose also helps to teach you how to be better the next time. Failure is an integral part of success. A while back I was interviewing a friend, and fellow speaker, Bruce Hale. He said that failure is just an unintended outcome. I love that attitude. The fact that you tried is what's important. You can attempt to predetermine the outcome, but you rarely control all of the variables. Success is often an unintended outcome as well. How many things have ended up better than you had planned? Those were unintended outcomes, too. One of my catering client's signature dish was the result of an accident.

Whether wedding and event DJ sales is your main job, or a means to an end, it all starts with you making a sale. This book will give you easy to use ideas that you can implement right away in your business. I don't know your sales ability, or how long you've been selling, but I know there are nuggets here for everyone. Let's get started.

CHAPTER 2

Ask better questions

Sales, simply put, is about asking better questions. As I said in the introduction, given the chance, your customers will tell you everything you need to know to make the sale. So what's getting in the way? Well, to be blunt, you are. You're the reason your prospects don't reply to your emails (they 'ghost' you). You're the reason your sales meetings take longer than they should. And you're the reason you don't close all of the sales you could. But don't fret, I'm not being hard on you, I'm the reason I don't close all of my sales, either. We all need to get out of our own way.

The challenge comes when you want to tell, when you should be listening. But listening is really hard. There's a big difference between hearing and listening. Very often they hear that you're talking, but they're not really listening to what you're saying. Have you ever been thinking about the next thing you want to say before the other person stops talking? You're not listening, are you? If you're going to say what you want to say, regardless of what the other person says, you can't be listening. If you were really listening, then what you say next would have a direct connection to what they're saying.

When you're speaking, everything you're saying, you already know. I'm not talking about coming up with a new idea, or a new phrasing. When you're talking to a customer, you're not going to learn what will make them buy your DJ, photo booth or lighting services. You're only going to learn that when you're asking them good questions and really listening to their answers.

The key to listening better is learning to be present, not just physically, but mentally. Listen not only to their words, but also their body language. Traci Brown is a body language and neurolinguistics expert. Her books and presentations help you "read" their body language, and show us how changing their physical body position can alter how they're receiving your message. If they have their arms crossed (in what I call the "you can't touch my wallet" pose), she says to give them a drink, or a pen, or a squeeze ball... anything for them to hold. The act of uncrossing their arms makes them more receptive to your message. In sales meetings, mirroring their body language makes them feel more comfortable and connected with you, on an unconscious level.

This applies to written conversations, too. In emails you can also "hear" their tone and energy, when you read not only the words, but how they were written. Learn to write the same things you would say if they were on the phone (since it seems they don't want to pick up the phone and call you these days). While that sounds simple, it's harder than it would appear. You were taught to write one way, and speak another. It's easy to fall into conversational speech when it's verbal, but once you start putting that on paper (or a screen) you start hearing your 8th grade grammar teacher changing your conversational style into a written, more formal style.

Gen Y, the Millennials, and Gen Z, who follow them, are digital natives. They've grown up with today's technology, so they're comfortable having a real conversation digitally. Whether you're also a Millennial, Gen X or a Baby Boomer, I know it's easier for most of you if they would just call you. But they don't, so you have to adapt to them, not the other way around. If your reply to their inquiry is to ask for the appointment or a phone call, right away, you're probably having limited success with that. You need to build a rapport first, and it's possible to do that without speaking with them.

If you could see a written transcript of a phone conversation you've had with a customer, would it have large blocks of you talking, or would be it be a lot of shorter, back and forths? More likely it would be shorter back and forth banter, with you asking a question and them answering.

When they ask you a question, how often do you ask a clarifying question before answering to make sure you understand why they're asking that particular question? Sales isn't about assumptions, it's about facts combined with emotions. I do a presentation on why entrepreneurs make emotional decisions. In my research I found that all decisions involve your emotions, some more than others. People who have damage to the part of the brain that controls emotions have trouble making even the simplest of decisions (what to eat, what to wear, etc.).

If you're selling entertainment and lighting for weddings and social events, emotions are going to play a strong part in their decision-making process. Learning how to ask better questions, ones that evoke emotions, can help you make that unconscious connection with your customers. As Bob Burg (no relation) famously said, *"All things being equal, people do business with, and refer business to, those people they know, like and trust."* (you'll be hearing that a lot in this book) Asking better questions can help you make that personal connection. Now let's look at what kinds of questions to ask and see some real examples.

CHAPTER 3

Yes or No vs. Open-Ended Questions

Should you ask Yes or No questions or open-ended questions, where they have to give you a longer answer? That depends upon the outcome you're working towards. A couple of really good Yes or No questions are *"Are you ready to reserve our photo booth for the bar mitzvah?"* or *"Have you already decided to have us DJ your wedding?"* With those types of questions, you're getting a direct answer to a direct question. The information you hear will tell you what to do next; hopefully to get out a contract and start writing.

If your Yes or No questions are more vague, you'll have to ask more questions to get closer to the sale. For example, asking *"Do you like our lighting?"* only gets you a yes or no answer. You won't know what it is they do, or don't like. And, more importantly, you won't know why. Getting to the WHY is the key to making that emotional connection. You already know that they want or need DJ services and/or lighting like yours, or you wouldn't even be talking/writing with them. Finding out their why comes from asking better questions.

Here are some examples of better questions to ask:

- Instead of asking *"Do you like our lighting?"* - ask *"What is it that you like about our lighting?"* - or - *"If you could change something about this lighting package, what would you change, and why?"*

- Instead of asking *"Do you have a preference for which music you want for your wedding?"* – ask *"Which songs are important to your families, and how would they make your wedding more special, and why?"*

- Instead of asking *"Do you have any songs you don't want us to play?"* – ask *"Which songs would you like us to avoid, and why?"* (with the why being the important part)

A WeddingWire survey showed that 88% of respondents trust online reviews as much as personal recommendations. That's right, they trust the words of people they'll never meet as much as people they work with, live near or worship with. They show the *results* of working with you. That's why I believe you should be using reviews and testimonials on all of your marketing pieces, and on every page of your website. I know that some of you have a testimonials page on your sites, but is anyone seeing it? In the website reviews that I do with single-op and multi-op DJs, companies just like you, we often look at your Google Analytics reports (or other website tracking). Almost every time we find that very few people are visiting those testimonials pages. So their site visitors are not seeing or reading all of those wonderful sentiments.

If you take a look at your analytics report, it will show you the pages that are visited the most. Those are the pages where you should have testimonials and reviews. That will give you the most impact. That's why I say you should have them everywhere. And so you don't think I'm a hypocrite, take a look at my websites, www.AlanBerg.com and www.YourPersonalSalesTrainer.com and see how I use them. I even have them on my business cards, bookmarks and promotional pieces.

Now that we know they love to read and trust those reviews, here's how you can use them in your questioning. Try asking *"If you could write the review of your wedding now, what would you want it to say?"* or *"When they go back to work on the Monday after your wedding, what do want your wedding guests to say to their friends and co-workers about your wedding?"* Don't influence their answer by suggesting anything (the ceremony, the dancing, the photo booth), let them think about it and reply. Some will reply immediately and others will be less emotive. For the ones that are less emotive, quieter, or shyer, instead of suggesting answers, help them with another question such as *"What thing, or things, are most important when choosing your _____ (DJ, photo booth, lighting...)?"*

I recently did on-site sales training for a venue group. A few days later I got an email from one of the sales associates, telling me how asking better questions had helped her with a sale. The bride told her that she, the sales associate, was the only one who actually asked them what they wanted for their wedding.

The key is to ask a better question so you get more information. That's information you can use to move them closer to the sale. You're helping both of you that way. You'll get more of their WHY, and they'll feel more connected to you because they feel you care more about their wants and needs. And, their wants and needs aren't your products and services, it's the results they'll get by choosing you.

Open-ended questions can get even the quietest and reserved customers to engage in conversation. The key is to find the things they're most passionate about. People are passionate about successful outcomes. They don't usually care how you get them there, as long as you do. They don't care how much you've invested in equipment, facilities or even training, if they don't want the outcome you're going to produce. They don't care about your environmental policies or smaller carbon footprint if they don't want the results you're going to provide. The key is to get them to want you, and only you, to provide the results. When they want you, they have to hire you, and only you, at your price, to get those results. That's the result we're going to work you towards with this book.

Here are more examples of better open-ended questions to help you understand their needs:

- What kind of music do you listen to when you're alone?
- Are there any special songs, or traditions that we need to honor at your wedding?
- What do the song choices mean to you?
- How do you want your wedding entertainment to make your guests feel?
- What have you seen at other wedding DJs that you didn't find here with us?
- What one thing do you absolutely have to have for your wedding entertainment?
- What have you seen at a friend or relative's wedding that you want for yours?
- Besides your first dance, what is the most important music choice for your wedding?

CHAPTER 4

Understanding your brand

I've had people ask me, when did I know I had a personal brand? It was while I was VP of Sales at The Knot, and their main public speaker on business topics at conferences. Event planners and conference promoters would ask The Knot to send someone to speak at their conference. The tipping point came when they started asking specifically if I could come and speak. They didn't want someone, they wanted me.

The same applies to you. If they can't perceive any difference between you and another DJ, MC or photo booth company in your market, they'll go with the lower-priced competitor. This is about their perception, not yours. That means that you have to be able to explain why you're the best person/company to get them to their desired outcome. You do not do this by bashing your competitors. You do this by providing them with a better customer experience. You do this by showing your value from the first exposure they have about you, be it in your online ads, on your business card, in your wedding show booth display, or on your website.

Your brand is defined by the words and phrases that your customers use when they talk about you to their friends, family, co-workers and yes, in their reviews and testimonials. Those are the words that others will use to decide whether or not they want to have you be a part of their wedding or event. That's why I stressed in the last chapter about you using those words in your marketing and on your websites. You don't want them to want *somoene* to DJ their wedding or event. You want them to specifically want *you* for their wedding or event DJ.

You can also use them in your email conversations with prospects. In my book *"Why Don't They Call Me? 8 tips for converting wedding and event inquiries into sales,"* one of the 8 tips is to keep your emails short. These days you should try to keep them to what will fit on one screen of their smartphone, as that's where they're most likely reading your email, while they're at work. We've all experienced getting a long email that we put aside to read later (if we get to read it at all). However, when we get a short email we tend to read it right away. If you want them to read and reply faster, write shorter emails.

A nice touch is to use reviews/testimonials in your emails that are specific to what they've asked, as a way to answer their questions. If someone asks *"What if my DJ gets sick on my wedding day?"* You could reply with *"Thanks for asking, while that has rarely happened, we are dealing with people and things happen, however, we have you covered for any situation. As a matter of fact, one of the only times it has come up, here's what Debbie, the bride, wrote in her review on WeddingWire: 'My original wedding DJ came down with the flu the night before our wedding, but Elite sent Heather and she did a fantastic job, everything ran smoothly and we had a great time.'* – So, you can see we're going to ensure the success of your wedding."

WeddingWire says, "*As common with most big purchases, 83% of searching couples like to hear what they should expect, not from the vendors themselves, but from past customers who've been in their position.*" If a customer is on the fence about a certain product or service, instead of you trying to convince them, show them reviews of satisfied customers that speak specifically about that product or service. For example, if they're not sure they want to spend for a duet entree, show them reviews that say: "*At first we weren't sure about spending the extra for the second monogram, but when we saw it in the room, we were so glad we did. So many of our guests commented on how amazing the room looked.*"

Recently at an industry conference, someone came up to show me their new business card. They had a few key words under their logo on the cards and they proudly proclaimed that they found those words in their reviews and testimonials after hearing me speak about this. The words that kept popping up defined their brand, so they started using them in their marketing.

Which words and phrases come up repeatedly in your reviews and testimonials? For some of you it's "professional" or "creative" or even "fun". When consulting with a bridal shop about their website, we went to WeddingWire to look for reviews to use on their site. The word "fun" kept popping up. I've worked with lots of bridal salons and I've never seen the word "fun" as the dominant brand word. I had only worked with them on phone/web consultations, so I hadn't been to their shop, but I already had a feeling of what it would be like. It would be a FUN experience! I knew that, and so do the brides who are checking them out through their reviews.

How is your entertainment company's brand defined by your customers? Don't just skim through your reviews. Really read them. Highlight the words and phrases that come up over and over. Those are your brand in the eyes of your customers and prospects. If there are negative words and phrases that come up repeatedly then you've uncovered a problem. You might get upset at reading them, but that's how you're perceived. If they say you're "unresponsive" then your idea of being responsive isn't aligned with your customers'. Learn to appreciate this free market research and you'll learn how to profit from it.

CHAPTER 5

Invest in your success

If you want customers to invest in you, you have to invest in your business first. I'm not talking about the obvious things like equipment, vehicles and staff. You need to invest in:

- Better branding
- Better marketing
- Better website
- Better communication skills
- Better sales skills
- Better networking skills
- and, of course, better technical & customer service skills

You can't expect people to invest in your DJ services, lighting or photo booth, for their weddings and events, if you aren't willing to lead the way. Where would you expect to find the best businesses in your market, on the last page of search results on sites like WeddingWire and The Knot, or the smallest booth in the back of a wedding show? Of course not! You'd expect to see them in prominent positions. The perception is that the most successful businesses will still be around when their wedding happens, be it 3 months or 15 months into the future. No matter whether they're a low-budget wedding or high-end gala, they want to know you're successful. Investing in your success makes you more attractive to prospective customers. People want to do business with successful businesses and people.

Can you tell when someone has hired a professional graphic designer to create their logo, business cards and marketing pieces? Of course you can. Can you tell when someone made their website themselves, versus hiring a professional web designer? I'll bet you can, and so can your prospects. Does your website look as professional as the entertainment services you're providing? What are you up against? You can't just look at your marketing and website in a vacuum, you have to see what the current competitive landscape looks like. We have to remember that they'll be seeing your marketing and website beside those of other companies, inside the events industry and outside. You don't have to have the most expensive or fanciest website and marketing, but you do have to be competitive. Staying competitive means investing and reinvesting in your success.

Let's start with your email address. There have been numerous articles that say, if you have a website, which I would hope everyone reading this book already does, then your email should be yourname@yourDJwebsite.com. If you're using Gmail, Yahoo, your ISP (internet service provider/cable company), or AOL for your business email you're sending the wrong message. Some people may interpret that as your not being full time, or not an established business.

Another benefit of using your own website for your email address is that, when you give someone your email address they have 3 things: your name, your email address and your website address. If you give them a Gmail or similar address, they only know your email. Haven't you ever had someone's email address and used it to go to their website? I'm sure you have and so have your customers and prospects.

What's the difference between an expense and an investment? Expenses are things you get value from, through their utility. These are things like your cell phone, rent, electricity and your work car/truck. In other words, you get what you pay for, no more, no less. Investments, by their nature, can provide you a return that's greater than their cost. If paying to have a larger facility will allow you to do larger weddings and events, making you more profit, that's an investment. If you're a DJ and your controller breaks, buying a new one is an investment, as you can't do events without one. However, if your controller is working fine and gets you the results you and your customers need, buying the newest model, just because it's cool, is an expense. I'm not saying you shouldn't buy it, but if you can't make any more money with it than you do now, it's not going to return you more than it's going to cost. At some point we all realize that we have enough equipment. The relentless pursuit of the latest gadget or shiny object is often just draining our bank accounts, not adding to them. The goal of this book is to help you sell more (so you can afford the cool stuff). Let's take a look at the steps to more sales.

CHAPTER 6

The 4 Steps to More Sales

For most of us, there are 4 steps to making more sales:

1. Get their Attention
2. Get the Inquiry
3. Get the Appointment
4. Get the Sale

Throughout this book we'll explore these and see how they can help you sell your DJ services, lighting and photo booths more. If our prospects don't know we exist, we can't make the sale. If they know we exist but don't inquire with us (email, phone, walking in…), we can't make the sale. If they inquire with us but don't make an appointment, whether in-person or virtual, we can't make the sale. And if we get to speak with and/or meet with them and they don't buy, we don't get to provide them with the products and services of which we're most passionate. Passion is likely the reason you started your DJ business, but if they don't buy you can't share that passion, and your talent with them. We'll break these down over the following chapters.

To get their attention, you need to be where they're looking for a DJ like you. That means being on the websites, at the wedding shows, and in the publications that they're using to plan their weddings, quinceañera, bar/bat mitzvah, etc.. That means making an investment in time and money, so you'll be seen at the time they view that site, go to that show or read that magazine. Then, you need to decide how you want to be perceived and how prominently you want to be seen.

Will taking a front page placement on The Knot or WeddingWire cost more than being on page 2, 3 or 5? Of course, but don't look at the cost without looking at the return. If the first-page ads are viewed a lot more than those on subsequent pages, which they almost always are, the higher investment could pay for itself many times over. You have to be willing to make the upfront investment, because you don't get the return without taking that leap of faith.

Live by the philosophy **"Go big, or go home"**. You can't take the smallest ad, or booth, and use that as a benchmark as to what a better placement would get you. All too often I see businesses trying to "test out" an ad by taking the lowest cost option and saying *"If this works I'll upgrade."* That's a flawed approach. When you buy advertising or a booth at a wedding show you're buying access to that audience. If you feel that audience is right for you, then you should want to be in the most visible place available. Make it so they can't miss you. Take the better ad and you can honestly say you gave it your best shot. While consulting with entertainment companies, I very often see that their WeddingWire tracking shows that taking the Spotlight position, the highest placement that appears first in that category, is getting them way more views and clicks to their site than any other available placement. They were certainly getting more value, even though they were paying the most. Taking the smallest ad is not getting a "taste" of what it would be like to have the better placement.

Another part of getting their attention is networking. There are countless local and national groups to help you connect with other wedding and event pros. Some are category-specific and others are open to all categories. Check in your area for local associations, so you can network within and outside your category. Here are some of the more popular, national groups:

- ABC - Association of Bridal Consultants
- ADJA - American Disc Jockey Association
- AfWPI - Association for Wedding Professionals Intl.
- ILEA - International Live Events Association
- NACE - National Association of Catering and Events
- NAWP - National Association of Wedding Professionals
- PPA – Professional Photographers of America
- WIPA – Wedding Industry Professionals Association

It's important to look outside your category for a few reasons. While learning to improve your technical skills is important, so is paying attention to what other businesses are doing, so you can improve your business skills – probably one reason why you're reading this book. Being technically proficient at something, but not making money at it, makes it either a hobby or a failing business. Learning to improve your business acumen allows you to do more of what you love, which are the creative and technical skills (planning fun weddings, mixing music, creating grand entrances, dreaming up fabulous décor, etc.).

Networking with other DJs may yield you some referrals, as when someone else is already booked for a date, or if you fill a particular niche they don't offer (speak a certain language, or have experience with specific ethnic traditions). Networking with those who get booked before you, has a greater chance of yielding referrals. In the wedding or event timeline, which categories get booked before you? Likely venues, caterers, planners, photographers, etc. Find them and network with them.

The key to networking and getting referrals is that people refer people they know, like and trust. You can't just show up with a handful of business cards and expect to get referrals. You have to show up, often, with an open hand, volunteer and become a resource for others. Then, once they know, like and trust you, they'll be more likely to refer you. From my experience, you're much more likely to get referrals not by asking, rather by showing with your actions, that you're deserving of those referrals. If you're new to a market, area or group, one of my best pieces of advice is to join a local group and volunteer to be the person to check in attendees to the events. You'll meet everyone who attends, others will see you helping out and you'll be making a great first impression. Each meeting you attend is an opportunity, not because you'll be asking for referrals. Rather, just by showing up, and participating, others will see the value you provide, and your attitude and commitment, both to that group and to the industry.

CHAPTER 7

Marketing is like a relay race

Now, let's focus on the next action you want your customers to take. Once you've gotten their attention, you want to get them to reach out to you and make an inquiry, whether via email, phone, walking in, or whatever other methods you use. I've often said that marketing is like a relay race, where runners pass a baton to the next runner, and then the next, until the last one finishes the race. If any of the runners drops the baton, the race is over for that team. Your marketing works the same way, moving your prospects forward from step to step, until you close the sale.

If you choose not to be on a particular website, or at a certain wedding show or expo, and there are viable prospects there, for dates you have open, you've dropped the baton. If you did take an ad, but on page 3, and that prospect didn't look past page 1, you dropped the baton by not upgrading to the first-page placement. If you didn't maximize the experience on your ad (better photos, messaging and branding), or if they don't like your website, or if you don't know how to communicate in a way that connects with your prospects (you want them to call you, they want to email), you've dropped the baton. If you get them in for an appointment, but don't show them why you're the best DJ or MC for their wedding or event, or if you don't close them on the first appointment and then you don't follow up with them, you've dropped the baton. The official term for the money you could have earned by not dropping the baton is Opportunity Cost, a concept I'll cover in a later chapter.

Don't get discouraged; if you're making any sales now you're obviously doing some things correctly. If your calendar is full with customers you want to do business with, who are paying the prices you want to get, then I'm really happy that you're reading this book. It shows your commitment to getting even better at sales, which is why your calendar is already full. However, if your calendar has open dates, or you're not profiting enough for your efforts, then reading this book should give you plenty of ideas on how to improve upon what you're doing now.

The key to getting their attention is being everywhere that prospects are looking for a DJ, lighting company or photo booth, like yours. If they're looking on certain websites, attending certain wedding or trade shows, reading certain blogs/magazines/websites and/or using particular social media channels, you should be there as well. But don't just jump into the deep end of the social media pool without having a plan for getting their attention and then, more importantly, getting them to take action. Success doesn't come from ideas. Success comes from taking action. Too many DJs spend hours upon hours on social media, with no return on their investment of time and money. Are you making any money from the time you spend on social channels? When I look at most DJ's social pages I see lots of posts by you, but not a lot of interaction by your audience. That's a sign that they're not really engaged with you. Are they paying attention to what you post? Are they being moved to interact?

Has your number of Friends or Likes gone up lately? Has it gone down? If it's gone down that's a really bad sign. It takes a lot for most people to Unfriend or Unlike you. If your number is going down, you had better take a look at what you said or did to turn off your audience. Similarly, if your number of Friends or Likes is going up, what are you doing to foster that? Whatever it was, do more of that. Then take a look and see if you're getting any "engagement" by your couples (pardon the pun):

- Are they Liking your posts? Good.
- Are they commenting on your posts? Even better.
- Are they going to your website, or contacting you directly to get more information? Excellent. That's exactly the action you want them to take.

You don't make any money directly from them Liking or Friending you. They have to contact you – the inquiry – for you to have a chance to make money from your social presence.

What I want you to realize is that it's not just one step from when they first find out about you, to making the sale. There are many steps. Getting their attention is an important step. Once they know you exist, you need to move them forward in the sales process. That's getting them to make an inquiry. So let's move on to that.

CHAPTER 8

Getting more inquiries

Now that you have their attention by advertising and marketing in the places where they're looking, and networking in the right circles, you want to get more of them to contact you. Getting more inquiries is about making it clear as to what action you want them to take, and then making it easy for them to take that action. This is not the time to be subtle. If you want specific action, make that action clear. But let's be realistic here, you want them to call you, as that would be easier for you, and they would rather email you. For some of you that's frustrating because you're also digital immigrants, like me.

Many of us are digital immigrants, because we know what it's like to do business without much of today's technology. I've come along willingly because I like technology. More importantly, I've learned to use the communication methods that my clients like to use, and so should you. Today's customers are digital natives, as are most of Generation Y (and all of Gen Z, which follow next). They've grown up in a world with personal computers, cell phones and email. They don't know what it's like to do business without them, so they're very comfortable having a real conversation through email, text and other electronic means.

Do you remember when Facebook Messenger first arrived? I wasn't happy about it. I thought that phone, email and texting was already stretching my limits. I certainly didn't need another communication channel. Then something interesting happened; I started to make money through Facebook Messenger. No one was paying me to use it. Clients and potential clients were contacting me through Facebook Messenger and hiring me to speak, buying my products and having me do consulting, mastermind days, on-site sales training and website reviews. I can attribute real dollars to those interactions, which continue today. Sure, if Facebook Messenger didn't exist, many of those same people would still contact me, or would they?

With Facebook Messenger they don't need our phone number or email address to contact us. If they just saw me at a conference, read a post of mine, saw me mentioned and tagged in a post, or just stumbled across my page, they can contact me. I've embraced Facebook Messenger because that's what my customers want to use. I appreciate that I can reach out to my thousands of Facebook friends and fans, without knowing their email addresses or phone numbers (since Facebook blocks most people's contact info these days). I also find it to be much more conversational than email. It's less formal and has less of a sense of urgency than texting. While I do reply when I see I've received a message, it's not as interrupting as a text message.

Here's a hard truth: no matter how long you've been in business, how many times you've been on TV, or how many weddings you've done, everyone does not know you. There's a new crop of weddings and clients every year. If they haven't had a need for your services before, they may not know you. Even if they've been to an event that you were a part of, they may not know it was you. They may have been to many other weddings and events before and since. Just because they enjoyed themselves doesn't mean they'll remember that it was you. Can you name the entertainment, floral decorator or photographer from the weddings and events you've attended as a guest? Marketing is a constant process. I'm often asked how you can stay busy. It's not doing one thing. It's doing many things.

Since many of you would prefer that all prospects would pick up the phone and call you, and we know that doesn't happen much anymore, don't make calling the main way to contact you. Most of your inquiries are coming in during the week, during the day, while your prospects are at work. The next most popular time is probably late at night. At both of those times they either can't call you (at work), or they figure you're not going to answer (i.e. if it's late at night).

When I speak about how to better handle email inquiries, I break it down to a common sense approach. If they had wanted to talk to you on the phone, they would have called you, during the day. So, stop trying to force a phone call on your initial email reply. You haven't earned their trust yet, and Gen Y (the Millennials), and Gen Z are more than a little phone-averse. As I mentioned earlier, they're perfectly comfortable having a real conversation through email, or text, or WhatsApp. It's your turn to learn to do that as well.

The simplest way to get a better response, is to learn to have the same conversation via email that you would have on the phone. You wouldn't grill someone on the phone with 5 questions at once, before giving them a chance to answer. You ask one question, and then, based upon their answer, you know what to ask next. If you're having a real conversation you wouldn't have a pre-set order of questions. You'd let the conversation zig and zag, leading the prospect to tell you everything you need to know to close the sale – but I'll speak more about that a little later.

If they want to email you, make it easier for them. Many of my clients, businesses just like yours, have put a short contact form on almost every page of their websites. Those who've done it have seen an increase in their number of inquiries. After adding a short contact form to every page of their site, one catering client got 2 1/2 times the number of inquiries as they did the prior year. If getting more inquiries is your goal, this is a relatively easy fix. Getting more inquiries is about having better conversions – getting more people who visit your website, or who are exposed to your marketing, to take action. Adding more calls-to-action on your marketing and on your website is key. Just having your phone number, email or web address is not a call-to-action. It's just data. Telling them why they're contacting you (what's in it for them), and then showing them how to contact you – and making it easy – will get more of them to do it.

CHAPTER 9

How many buying signals have happened before you get an inquiry?

Buying signals are things people say, or do, to show you that they're interested. When a prospect calls, emails or texts you for the first time, how many buying signals have already happened? It could be 3, 4, 5 or more. Consider that when a couple goes to the WeddingWire or The Knot website, they've already decided that they need things for their wedding. That's a buying signal. Actually, researching websites to find information for their weddings is a buying signal, so going to those sites might be their 2nd or 3rd buying signal. Next they go to your market and then the DJ, Lighting & Décor or Photo Booth category, two more buying signals. Depending upon which placement level you've taken, they may or may not see your thumbnail image. If they do, and click on it, that's another buying signal. If they like what they see (photos, videos and awards) and read (text, reviews and peer endorsements), they may decide to contact you there. It's also likely they'll visit your website, which is another buying signal. Once at your website, if they like what they see and read, they may decide to contact you, another buying signal. So, you can see that getting the inquiry is your first visible buying signal, but far from their first one.

How many other entertainment companies in your market will never get an inquiry from that same prospect? Whether they were advertising in the same places, at the same level, or not, they didn't make the cut. At some point along the way that prospect decided to scratch them off the list, at least the short list of businesses whom they've contacted. Maybe they didn't like their photos, or reviews. Maybe they made it to their website, but they didn't like it enough to contact them. Regardless of how many they've looked at, they've only contacted a small subset, and you are on that list.

Some of you are thinking that they're reaching out to a large number of DJs. After all, it's really easy to copy the email they send to the first DJ, and send it to dozens or more businesses. While that's true, they don't reach out to dozens, or more, because they don't want to field the replies. They may have looked at dozens of online profiles and websites, but by the time they reach out to you, they've already done a lot of filtering. Some of that filtering was done by you, by choosing not to be on that website, at that wedding show, or not optimizing your website for the keywords they used when searching. The rest of the filtering is by the prospect using whatever criteria is important to them. For some it's your photos and videos. For others it's your reviews. For others it could be your website's first impression on them.

Whatever the filtering process, when you get an inquiry, you've made it to their short list. It's now your sale to win or lose. They're going to hire a DJ, why not you? You still have to get the next steps right, but you should have the confidence to know that you're speaking with, or writing to a prospect that most of your competition will never even know exists. Confidence is attractive in life and in business. Cockiness, or arrogance, on the other hand, is a sure way to turn off most prospects. Confidence comes from preparation. Cockiness comes from a sense of entitlement, that you deserve the sale. You don't deserve the sale because you've made it this far. You still need to earn their trust from your actions.

So, the next time you get an inquiry, even one that only asks how much you charge, start with a sincere *"Thank you"*. There are many other DJs, MCs, lighting companies and photo booths in your market who will never get a chance to speak to them. Appreciate the opportunity you're being given, even if they begin with a price question.

CHAPTER 10

Creating better calls-to-action

A little earlier I referred to having better calls-to-action, but what does that mean? Simply put, instead of just asking them to call, email, text or fill out your contact form, be more specific about the kinds of action they can take. Calls-to-action should be contextual, so they're just the next thought within a section of text. As a matter of fact, when I speak about having better web pages, having a strong call-to-action is the most important element. You can grab their attention, engage them both visually and with your words, but if you don't tell them what to do next, and make it easy to do so, fewer people will take the action you want.

Strong calls-to-action tell your prospects what to do in order to get the outcomes they desire. If you're a wedding DJ, show them pictures of real couples and their guests, enjoying the wedding, dancing and smiling, surrounded by their smiling family and guests. Talk to them about how happy their guests will be, and support that with quotes from real couples talking about how their guests couldn't stop talking about what a great party it was. Your next step is to tell them how to get that result *"To have an amazing wedding, with your family and friends having the time of their lives, call, text or contact us today, 214.555.1212, WeddingFun@AustinWeddingDJ.com."*

Always include a link to your contact page and/or your email, and put your phone number (make it so they can click to dial on mobile), no matter how many times it's already on the page. Don't make them search for it. If you say "call", put your phone number. If you say "email" or "contact us", include a link. If you say text us, make sure a textable phone number is included. If you have a short contact form on that page (which is a really good idea if you want more inquiries) then refer to it. Try using a call-to-action that refers to the form. Something like this *"If you want your wedding to be romantic, fun and memorable, call me, email me or use the short form on this page, 555.422.6362."*

Be sure to keep your contact forms short. You want to ask only what you need to know to start a conversation, not everything you'll need to know to make the sale. When any of us is presented with a long contact form we often decide not to fill it out, even if all of the fields aren't required. When we see a short contact form, we're much more likely to complete it. For every field you add to your form, you're likely to lose some legitimate prospects. I had a bride once tell me that when someone asks for her mailing address on a form, she won't complete it at all. She finds it intrusive, and she doesn't understand why you need her address to answer her questions, or to give her a quote. You know what? She's right. You don't need her physical address to have a conversation with her. As a matter of fact, all you need to start a conversation through your website, is their name and email address. You can, and should, ask for a phone number, but with this generation, you really don't need it.

Even if you have a long form, and many people complete it, there are way more who looked at it and decided to move on to someone else. Besides, if you ask them all of the questions you need on a form, you're eliminating the chance to answer their questions and concerns with emotional text, to show them why you're the right choice for them. Not someone like you. Specifically, you and your company. All you're left with to talk about is price, the one thing you don't want to talk about, yet. Remember, they can always find someone who will do what you do, for less money than you're asking. If they can't tell the difference between you and someone else who charges less, then they should hire them. If you can get them to want you to do their ceremony sound, or be their DJ, they have to hire you, at your price. You're DJ and MC services are not available anywhere else, at any other price. You're not available anywhere else, at any other price.

So, make your calls-to-action in the context to what you've written just before that. Include the outcome(s) they want, and include the specific action you want them to take, for them to get that outcome. Using visuals cues can help you get more conversion. Buttons that say *"Click here to start planning your fantastic wedding entertainment"* or *"Ready to get started with amazing lighting? Click here!"* or *"Click here to schedule your personal meeting with Paul,"* will get you more conversion than just listing your contact information.

Another way to put a call to action is to list and number their next steps. This can be done with buttons or other visual cues:

"Here's what you should do next:
1) First click here to see the wedding DJ packages
2) Next click here to check our date availability for your wedding
3) Then click here, or call to contact one of our friendly and talented wedding pros, 770.555.1212"

The key is to have them everywhere, so there's a relevant call-to-action in front of them, when they've seen, read or heard enough to want to take the next step (even if that next step is asking about price). The photos on your pages will get noticed before the words. You should also try to make some of those photos into clickable links to relevant pages. For instance, if you have a photo that shows off the creative way you light a room, put text on the photo that says *"See how the right lighting choices can enhance your wedding's theme and décor – click here"*, and then link that photo to your lighting info page. If you got their attention with that image, let them click the image to move them forward, closer to connecting with you. You can see that some of your calls-to-action are internal, leading to other pages on your site, and some are external: calling, emailing, texting, using live-chat, or filling out your contact form.

CHAPTER 11

Why do they always ask "How much?"

Why do they often ask you *"How much do you charge?"* in their very first inquiry? The short answer is that they don't know what else to ask you. They've probably never shopped for a DJ before, so they're not equipped to ask you better questions. We all do that when we're the customer buying something new. When we don't know what else to ask, we default to the one common denominator, which is price. They know that at some point you're going to want some of their money, and they understand money, so they ask *"How much..."*. They don't think it's a bad question. If they had a better question they would have asked it first.

When we're buying something we understand, we ask better questions before we ask about price. After all, if it doesn't satisfy our technical or emotional needs, price won't matter. If you need a chandelier with certain specifications, a ligthing truss of a certain size, or a vehicle with a certain capacity, you ask those technical questions first. If your technical needs aren't being met, you'll move on and keep looking. Price doesn't matter because you haven't checked off all of the other important boxes on your must-have, or would-like-to-have list. Once you know that your technical and emotional needs are being met, then you ask about price.

I'm guilty of this too, when we were shopping for window tinting for our new home. We had just purchased a baby grand piano, and I wanted to protect it, so it wouldn't get damaged by the sun's UV rays – which is why I never got my grandmother's piano. After doing a Google search for *"Central NJ residential window tinting for UV protection"*, I found a few sites that appeared to have what I needed. I already knew from their sites that they were in my area, did residential window tinting, and had UV tinting film.

As none of them had pricing information on their sites, just like your prospects I emailed 3 companies. Having never purchased window tinting before, I had no easy way to frame this purchase (compare it to prior experiences). With only 1 quote I wouldn't know if the price was fair, or not. If I get 2 quotes and they're far apart, I still won't know who's right. With 3 quotes I get a better handle on the price range. I don't go with the lowest quote, just because it's the lowest. I go with the one that will fulfill my needs, from a company I trust, at a fair price. Historically, I rarely go with the lowest price.

When it came time to email them (it was 9:30 p.m. on a

Saturday night, so I didn't call) I stared at my keyboard, trying to think of a good question to ask them. I already knew that they were in my area, did residential and UV tinting. The only other question that came to mind was *"How much is it to UV tint the windows?"* I knew that there must be a better question, I just couldn't think of one. So, reluctantly, I emailed the 3 companies, *"How much does it cost to UV tint windows?"* I now realize what a stupid question that was. I hadn't told them how many windows I needed tinted. I hadn't told them the size of the windows. I hadn't told them how high up some of the windows were. I hadn't told them that I have a homeowner's association (HOA) that has rules regarding window tinting. In other words, just as when you get a cryptic email asking about price, there was no way they could give me a price... but I asked the question anyway.

Sounds familiar, doesn't it? When it comes to weddings and socail events, most prospects don't know what to ask you. Yes, they have technical and emotional needs, they just don't know how to express them to you, yet, especially if you're the first one they've reached out to in your category. Don't get angry when they ask about price, be happy that you're having a conversation with them at all. Think about how many other entertainment or lighting companies in your market will never get to have a conversation with them. Think about how many buying signals they've already shown by getting to this point.

Think about all of the couples who bought your top package or service. How many of them asked about price first, or early in the conversation? Probably quite a few of them. When they ask you about price early in the conversation it doesn't mean they can't afford your services. It doesn't mean they're price shopping. It doesn't mean they want your bottom product or package. It doesn't mean they won't spend more. It simply means they don't know what else to ask you at this point. Your first thought should be one of gratitude for being able to converse with them at all. That's what feeds your family, pays the bills, and allows you to use your passion to make so many couples' wedding days better than they've imagined. Say *"Thank you for considering us for your wedding DJ."* Next we'll talk about how you can better handle these pricing questions.

CHAPTER 12

4 ways to handle pricing questions and pricing on your website

How do you handle that pesky *"How much do you charge?"* question, before you're able to actually answer it in an email, on your website, at a wedding show, and in an appointment? I'm going to share with you 4 ways you can handle the price question, and you can choose what's right for you, and your business in each situation.

1) Tell them – if there's only one price for that particular product or service, you could choose to just tell them. However, never tell them what they're going to get, without telling them why they should get it from you. It's the why that separates you from everyone else in your market and category. If they perceive the value to be the same from another company who has a lower price, they'll choose them, and they should. When you're the customer, you don't pay more unless there's good reason. Why should your customers pay more for you? I've touched on the why a little earlier in this book, and I'll expand on it again later, as it's critical to making more sales.

After you tell them, always ask for the sale. Here's how you can use this: "*Thanks for asking, a photo booth would be a great addition to your event. It's only an additional $X. Would you like me to add that to your event order?*"

2) Don't tell them – Most of you reading this don't want to talk about price, at least not yet. There are way more important factors than price when deciding on their DJ, MC, lighting or photo booth, and you want your chance to tell them all of the great things you can do for them and their wedding or event. The reality, according to a WeddingWire survey, is that 88% of couples are looking for pricing information before they reach out to you. Companies that don't have any pricing information on their websites will get less inquiries. You don't have to have every last pricing detail, but they're looking for some idea of price. So if you choose not to put any pricing information, you had better acknowledge that they're looking for it, or have asked about it, and then tell them why it's not there, and how to get a price quote.

Here's what I call "the phrase that pays": "*Thanks so much for asking. I don't want to leave out anything that's important to you, or have you pay any more than you should, to get everything you need and want for your wedding entertainment.*" Follow that with "*So, if it's OK, I'll ask you a few questions so I can work you up a quote that has only the things you want and need." And then you'll ask them one, low-commitment question, not 3 or 4 or 5 questions. You're having a conversation now, so make it a conversation and not an interrogation.

On your website, a variation of this would be *"I'm sure you'd love to know how much it's going to cost for your wedding entertainment, and we would love to tell you. Since everything for your wedding will be customized for you, it's hard to just throw out a number. We don't want you to pay any more than you should, to get everything you need and want for your wedding entertainment. So, to get a personalized quote for your wedding just call, text or email one of our friendly wedding specialists today, 305.555.1212 and we'll be happy to prepare a quote for you."*

3) **Starting price** – This is my least favorite way to start a pricing conversation. The first number they see or hear is the number they expect to pay. Unless the price your typical customer pays is close to that starting price, I wouldn't use this method. When you're the customer, and you see *"Prices start at…"* what are you thinking? Are you thinking that your price will be close to that starting price? Or, are you thinking that you'll pay some multiple of that number, maybe double, triple, or even more. You're starting a relationship with this couple. It should be based upon trust and honesty.

On the other hand, if most customers actually do pay close to your starting price, then it's fine. I consult with an event venue which is rented out for weddings. There really aren't many variables that can change the price, so when they say *"Venue rental for weekend weddings starts at only $7,700"*, that's what most couples will actually pay. Their range is small, as the highest package is only $1,500 more (not double, or triple, as with many other businesses).

4) Price range - Almost every DJ reading this book can, and probably should, quote a realistic price range. You don't need a data scientist to find your price range. If I were consulting with your business, I'd have you make a spreadsheet of all of the weddings you've done in the prior 12 months. We'd sort that list lowest to highest and we'd have your range. If the lowest one(s) don't represent a typical customer (like a Tuesday wedding in an off month), you can eliminate that one. Do the same for the highest one. If you got an amazing, top dollar wedding, but it doesn't represent your typical customer, you can leave that off your range as well. What you're left with is a realistic range of your prices. Then you can put on your website, or in an email *"Creative and fun weddings range from $X to $XX. To get an idea of how much your wedding entertainment will cost, call, text or email us today, 314.555.1212."*

Take a closer look at the numbers and very often another range will appear within the list. If you're like most businesses, you'll find that a big chunk of your customers fall within an even tighter price range. The services/products they got might be very different, but what they paid was similar. This is very common for companies like yours, where every event is very different. While each wedding or event will be very different, the price that each customer ultimately will actually pay is likely to fall within a noticeable range.

When you uncover that tighter range you can now quote in an even better, more transparent way *"Prices for wedding entertainment run from $A to $Z (your lowest to highest price), with our most popular packages being $D to $L (the range that most customers pay). To get a quote for your wedding call, text or email us today, 919.555.1212. "* You're satisfying the 88% who want to get some idea of pricing, without actually telling them how much their wedding services/products will cost. If you read the forums where couples chat with each other about their weddings, this is all they really want. They don't want you to dodge the price question. They don't want you to be evasive. They want you to acknowledge that they're asking and give them a ballpark idea of what they'll pay.

Many entertainment companies (single-op and multi-op)

have told me that after putting a realistic price range on their websites, their number of inquiries has dropped, significantly. That can be scary, at first, until you realize that those other leads were the ones who probably didn't have a big enough budget. When the quality of the leads goes up, and your sales go up, as has been the case for so many others, you'll have more time to spend with better-qualified prospects. That's a win-win.

If you want to expand upon this and have different price ranges for your DJ services, for different times of the year, or other variables, that's fine. Transparency will only help you. Oh, and if you're thinking that you don't want to put price on your website so your competitors don't see them, I have news for you. They already know your prices. They've either "secret-shopped" you, or one of your prospects showed them your pricing. The worst reason for not putting price is to hide it from your competition. They can copy your prices; they can try to copy your brand and look; but, they can never be you. Let's focus next on what you're really selling.

CHAPTER 13

What are you really selling?

I mentioned earlier that you need to tell them why they should choose you for their wedding or event. That's because, in writing, "what" you do looks pretty similar to what every other DJ or MC can do for them. The thing is, what you're selling is not your products or services. You're selling you, and your team, providing the results of choosing you to provide those products and services. Other businesses can sell similar, or sometimes, exactly the same things. If the prospect can't perceive any difference between what you're providing and another DJ who has a lower price, then you lose the sale. They have to perceive you to be providing a higher value or they won't pay more. Value is not just price. Value is the sum of the experience of doing business with you and a lot of intangible items (personality, response time, whether they like or trust you, etc.).

For example, whether you have 1-year experience performing at weddings, or 20 years, a bullet point list of "what" you're going to do for your couples looks pretty much the same:

- Experienced, professional DJs and MCs
- Arrange planning meetings with you
- Review your ceremony and venue setup
- Bring the latest equipment and music
- Coordinate a timeline with your other vendors to ensure everyone is where they're supposed to be, when they're supposed to be there
- Etc.

There are 100 other DJ in your area that say the same things. What does your list look like? Does it look like every other DJ's? Have you even looked at their websites to see what they're saying? While there's nothing inherently wrong with saying these things, there's also nothing unique about it. You don't want to blend in to a sea of mediocrity, where the only thing separating you from the others is price.

So, how do you do it better? I'm glad you asked! What if your bullet point list was the outcomes they could have if they choose you? Here's how that would that would look:

When you choose Acme Entertainment for your wedding, you'll always get:
- fun, creative music selections for your wedding
- innovative lighting choices to make your wedding day special
- the right music, at the right time, to leave your guests thrilled

Doesn't that sound better than *"Experienced DJs, choice of music..."*? Of course it does. Here's another example:

When you choose The Entertainment Masters for your wedding you'll always get:
- a packed dance floor, filled with your friends and family
- amazing lighting to enhance your theme
- ear-to-ear smiles from the fun you're all having

Doesn't that sound like a DJ you'd want at your wedding? I'll bet it does. If you want to take it a little further you can expand those descriptions, using more visual and emotional words, like this:

When you choose Laurelwood DJs for your wedding, you'll always have:
- someone who'll listen to your ideas and bring them to life
- colors, sights and sounds that bring a multisensory experience to your wedding
- design choices to enhance your theme and décor
- a DJ who's the supporting cast in your wedding production... you're the star
- and of course you'll have an amazing time, tired feet from dancing all night and happy guests

Can you feel a personality in that list? If you make a list like this, allow your personality to come through. After all, it's your personality they'll experience when they speak with or meet with you, so let them get a feel for it here. Here's another example that shows the personality of this business:

Come to Entertainment by Emily and you'll experience:

- friendly music consultants - we love helping you find the right choices
- a relaxed planning atmosphere - it's stressful enough, you don't need more
- lots of amazing lighting choices – don't worry, we'll help you find the perfect one
- in-house planning assistance - we aren't happy with your timeline, until you are

This list takes very familiar bullet list items and editorializes them, in a friendly, conversational way. What feeling do you get about that entertainment company? You've never visited them, but you're already getting a feeling for what it will be like, and it feels like it would be a good experience. Use bullet lists like this on your websites, in your marketing materials and even in your communication with prospects. You want to look and sound different because you are different.

I mentioned earlier that your brand is defined by the words and phrases customers use when they talk about you to their friends, and in their reviews and testimonials. You should use them on your website to support the things you're saying. Another way to use them is to make an even better bullet point lists of outcomes. After all, a real customer, talking about their real outcome is the best testimonial of all. I know a lot of wedding pros who bring former customers to their wedding show booths to talk to the couples who come by. You can't describe what you can do for them as well as someone who's already been on the receiving end.

So, what if you took those reviews and made a bullet list using those wonderful, emotive words? What would that look like? Here are some examples I made using real wedding DJs, and their real reviews. I went to their storefronts on The Knot and WeddingWire websites and took sound bites from the first 3 reviews:

What can you expect when you choose Remarkable Receptions for your wedding DJ?:
- *"We told Rich what we wanted the atmosphere to be and he gave us that and more."* — Karen K, Charlotte, NC
- *"The best DJ/MC ever!! Rich set the tone for such a loving and romantic day."* - Ashley M, Raleigh, NC
- *"The love story was so intimate, romantic, personal and nothing anyone has ever seen/heard before. IT WAS AMAZING! "* — Molly R, Marvin, NC

Here's another one:

Why choose Bill Hermann for your wedding?
- *"We loved Bill so much, we hired him as not only our DJ, but our officiant! Bill was worth every single penny."* — Erin F., Edina, MN
- *"Bill was simply amazing!! He made our wedding reception unique and special for both myself and my now husband, as well as all of our guests."* — Jenny F., St. Paul, MN
- *"He has an amazing way of captivating the room and making everyone really celebrate all the love that is present."* — Susan G., Minneapolis, MN

I made these using their 3 most recent reviews, without digging for even better quotes. Find all of your great quotes by doing an online search for *"Your Company Name Reviews"* i.e. *"Elite Entertainment Reviews"* or *"MB Events Reviews."* First of all, you might be surprised to find reviews on sites that you didn't know about. Next, really read the reviews to find those great words and phrases that describe the outcome, emotion and value of doing business with you. You'll likely end up with way more quotes than you can use. You may end up with so many that are specific to particular parts of your business, that you can make different bullet lists, with specific quotes, for different pages/services. I use lists like this on many pages on my website. We can't say many of the things that our customers say, and they say it with an emotion and passion that is unique to them.

Using your real reviews, and putting attribution - first names, with their city/state, and if you want, their venue and its city/state - adds credibility to their words. It can also help incrementally with your search engine optimization (SEO) as reviews often use some of your main keywords: wedding, DJ, lighting, photo booth, etc. Any time you can mention a city and/or state, or venue name, can help when someone does a search for someone like you, and includes that city or venue name. Since your business doesn't happen in one location, and your customers come from many locations, using their city/state and/or venue name with their testimonials sends the subtle message to your prospects that people just like them, use you for their weddings. All of this can help you convert more of your website traffic to make inquiries. Let's look at how you can get more appointments.

CHAPTER 14

Getting more appointments

Now that you've gotten their attention, and turned that attention into more inquiries, how can you get more appointments? The first thing to realize is that, these days, an appointment means more than just an in-person, face-to-face meeting. A pre-arranged phone meeting is an appointment. A Skype, Zoom or Facetime call or Google Hangout is an appointment. I use Join.me or Zoom to do most of my website reviews and consultations. With many platforms you can invest in a higher level so it's branded with your logo, photo and personalized URL. You can share your screen with your clients so whatever you see, they see. You can talk either on the phone or through your computers, and with the some versions you can even record the entire session, so the client can review it later, or forward it to people who weren't on the call. I've done these with people across town, and around the world. I once had a client in Key West, Florida, and her web designer in New Zealand, on the same call. My clients like the recording feature, so they don't have to write everything down.

Do you have to meet with them in person, or do you just want to? I consult for a DJ client who does all of his appointments through Google Hangouts. He says he almost never meets with his clients in person anymore. He's comfortable with it, and so are they. It's also convenient if there are people who need to be in the appointment who aren't in the same location. When you take travel time and geography out of the equation, you've lowered the barrier to them meeting with you.

I did a DJ Mastermind Day in Hamilton, Ontario with ten DJs. Nine of the ten insisted that they had to meet with a customer to close the sale. The other company did business in Toronto, but was based in Nova Scotia, hours away. They've been doing their appointments, and making their sales, remotely, for many years. That saves both they and their clients time and allows them to "meet" with them much sooner. It's a self-fulfilling belief. If you think you can sell them without meeting them in person, you're right. And, if you think you can't, you won't, because you've already decided it won't work. Hint...it does work!

A couple of weeks after doing a presentation on better emailing techniques, an attendee (a DJ) emailed me to say that he had written two contracts that week, without meeting in person, or speaking on the phone to either couple. He wrote one through email conversations and the other through Facebook

Messenger conversations. He said that he simply wrote what he would have said if he were on the phone with them, including any editorializing. Editorializing is when they say something and you add complimentary or visual words. For example, if they tell you their wedding date is May 22nd, you might say, *"Terrific, we still have that open and that's a beautiful time of year at your venue. The gardens are in full bloom, which is great for your wedding photos."* Leaving out the editorializing you'd simply say *"Terrific, we're available."*

It's hard to break the habit of how you've been writing. Once you do, you'll have much better luck converting inquiries to appointments and sales. I know that many of you are still skeptical that you can have the entire sales meeting virtually, or even in writing. It's a leap of faith, and one that many have done successfully. However, if you still feel you need to speak to them on the phone and/or in person, here's some good advice: start the conversation using whatever method they've used to reach out to you. If they email you, email them your reply. If they text you, text them back. If they call you (hallelujah), call them back. Then, after a few successful, short, back and forth exchanges say, something like, *"Hey, Chris, if it's easier for you, we could have a quick call. Can you talk now, or is there a better time?"* If he says *"Yes"*, then have the call. If he/she says he can't talk now then say *"Hey, I get it, I know it's tough to talk while you're at work, would this evening or tomorrow at lunch time work better for a quick call?"* If he/she agrees to a call, great. If not then be prepared to continue the conversation via email, or however you're now talking. If you try to force a call, or face-to-face meeting, especially early in the process, you're going to turn off many prospects. Don't believe me? How many of your inquiries ghosted you (went nowhere after your first or second reply)?

Notice that you gave him a choice of two each time. If you want someone to make a quicker decision don't leave it open-ended. It's hard to choose when there are too many choices, or when the choices are unlimited. This works when making appointments and when trying to close sales. They can always suggest a different answer, which is fine. If you suggest two days and times, they could always say, *"Those don't work, how about Thursday at 7pm?"* They can't make a decision until you help narrow their choices down to one or two. This method works in your personal life as well. Just try asking your friends where they want to go for dinner. You'll hear *"I don't know, where you do want to go?"* Twenty minutes later you're still trying to decide where to go (sound familiar?). Instead, if you say *"Do you want to go to Café Mumbai or Pete's Pizza?"*, you'll already be on your way.

Let your conversations evolve so that the appointment, whatever form it takes, is just the natural next step. Try something like this, *"Laurie, since we have your date available, you know the price, and I know we can make your wedding great, the only thing left is for you to come out* and meet us to see that we're a good fit. Did you want to come out this evening, or is tomorrow better?" (notice how we give them 2 choices) Or, if you're getting lots of great buying signals, you could say, *"Laurie, we have your date available, you know the price, and I know we can make your wedding great. Would it make sense to get your date reserved now?"* What's the worst that could happen? She could say, *"No, we're not ready yet."* To which you could reply *"Oh, I'm sorry, I was getting so excited about doing your wedding. What other questions do you have that we haven't already discussed?"* You see that her saying "No..." doesn't stop the conversation. It's just a speed-bump on the road to the sale. The fact that you're still having a conversation is a good buying signal. Remember, if you're having a conversation with them, they're probably going to buy your product or service from someone... why not from you?

If you learn to have better conversations you're likely to get more appointments. In the beginning of a relationship the customer should be doing more of the talking. You should be asking good questions that get them talking about what's important to them. As I said earlier, given the chance a prospect will tell you everything you need to know to close the sale. You just have to guide them along with great questions, and then really listen to their answers. I hope you're already getting some ideas you can use, right away, to improve your conversion. Now, on to one of my favorite topics – being happy versus being right!

CHAPTER 15

Do you want to be happy or right?

One of my favorite mantras to live by is: *"I've learned in business, and in life, that I'd rather be happy and successful, than be right."* If I have to prove that I'm right, that means someone else has to be wrong. If I tell my wife that she's wrong about something (which she rarely is), how is that going to work out for me? If I tell a customer that they're wrong, how is that going to work out for me? The lifetime value of a customer relationship is the amount of money that you will earn over the life of that relationship, from that customer and from their referrals. When a customer has a problem, that lifetime value gets paused, not stopped. If you handle their issue quickly, and to their satisfaction, the lifetime value not only continues, it could be higher. Customers will usually forgive you getting something wrong, as long as you make it right, quickly.

I've heard countless examples of DJs and entertainers who have offered customers more than would seem warranted to make them happy, and then they were rewarded with referral business, possibly more referral business than they would have gotten had nothing gone wrong. I know the owner of a DJ company with seven DJ's. Every Monday morning he calls every customer from the weekend, if he wasn't personally at their event, to see how things went for them. On one Monday he called a mother who had hired their company to DJ her young son's birthday party. The woman expressed that she wasn't happy with the performance of the DJ. He listened and apologized (two of the most important things you can do) and then offered her a partial refund. She appeared to be satisfied... but he wasn't. He went to a popular toy store and bought a gift card and a note card. He wrote an apology in the notecard, something to the effect of, *"I'm sorry that everything wasn't exactly the way you had expected for your son's party. Please buy him a gift from us"* and put the gift card in the envelope with it. He hand-delivered the envelope to her house. Within two weeks he had gotten two referrals from her that booked him for events. A few months later he called to tell me he had heard that I was telling his story. I asked if he wanted me to not tell it anymore and he said, *"No, it's fine, I just wanted you to know that I have booked 3 jobs now from that event, not two!"*

Another entertainment company told me that his company has a 100% satisfaction guarantee. A groom called after his wedding to say that something hadn't gone as expected.

After listening and apologizing, the owner asked the groom where to send the refund check. The groom said "*You don't have to give us back all of the money.*" The owner reiterated that they have a 100%, money-back guarantee, and since everything wasn't to their satisfaction with the entertainment they were refunding the entire amount. The owner told me that they, too, had gotten at least two referrals who booked them from that event. I asked him if anyone abused their 100% satisfaction guarantee and complained, even if nothing went wrong? He said "*You would think they might, but it hasn't happened, at least not yet.*"

Both of these examples show how a little short-term pain (giving the refunds), can lead to long-term gain. Had they not handled their situations well, it very well could have led to poor reviews, which could have cost them other business. I once had the owner of a multi-op wedding DJ company approach me at a conference, to tell me the story of a wedding where the power went out (not his fault). The couple went to the DJ at the event and demanded a refund. The DJ wasn't an owner and had no authority to give a refund. It's certainly questionable as to whether a refund was due, given the situation. The DJ would have kept playing but the wedding couldn't have gone on without power, even if he had backup power for his equipment. The customer wrote an email to the owner of the DJ company demanding a refund, and threatened to post 1-star reviews on the top wedding sites if he didn't comply. Instead of taking a deep breath, trying to put himself in their shoes (their wedding was ruined), and trying to appease the customer, he wrote them back a stern email saying that no refund was warranted as it wasn't his fault the power went out. The customer went and posted the negative reviews, exactly as they had said (or threatened). Now, the owner of the DJ company was standing before me asking how he could make those bad reviews go away. I asked him how much he would be willing to pay to erase them. Was it more than they paid him for the wedding? He said *"Absolutely."* I said *"So, now you're willing to pay that much. Why weren't you as willing when they first came to you with their issue?"*

He let his emotions get the best of him. Yes, they were bordering on extortion. He called their bluff and he lost. Had he called me before writing back to them I would have told him to think long-term, not short-term. I hope this never happens to you, but if it does, remember that you have an unhappy customer, and your first mission is to make them happy. Try to see it from their side, as if you were the customer. Think about what you would want to happen, and then act appropriately. Now, let's look at how to have better appointments.

CHAPTER 16

Having better appointments

Regardless of where you meet them, set the scene. First impressions are lasting impressions. When I do on-site sales training for a venue, caterer, DJ or any wedding or event business, one of the things I'll do is have you sit me down where the customers wait when they arrive. Especially if they arrive early and you're not yet available. When someone has been sitting for more than a few minutes they start to look around. What do they see? Is there a large screen monitor playing a slide show of images and videos from real events? Are they reading and seeing testimonials and videos? Or are they seeing broken ceiling tiles, chipped paint and wallpaper seams that are lifting? I'll also go into the restroom and look around. Is the garbage pail full of paper towels? Are the soap dispensers empty? Is there a garbage pail by the bathroom door so you can use your hand towel to open the door? This isn't nitpicking, it's important. You don't get credit for getting it right, but you lose points for getting it wrong. No one is going to congratulate you on having all of the light bulbs working in your office, but they will notice the bulbs that are out. That signals a lack of attention to detail and thoughts of deferred maintenance – what else may be wrong and what might you miss that their guests might notice at their wedding.

This is important when you're not a venue, and the guests won't ever visit your business. People want to do business with successful businesses. They want to know that you're going to be around when their wedding comes, months or a year (or more) later. They also want to know that your attention to detail is high. Signs of deferred maintenance are unnecessary red flags. You have to instill in your team that it's everyone's job to notice, and to report or fix these things.

If you're having a virtual appointment (Skype, Zoom, Google Hangout, FaceTime, Join.me, etc.) and you'll be using a web cam, watch your lighting and make sure your background isn't distracting. If you have a bright window behind you it can create a silhouette, making you look like you're in the witness protection program. If you have a window to the side, as I do, you can use window blinds, and lighting that allows you to dim and adjust the lighting as necessary for the conditions. Pay attention to what's behind you. Reduce the visual distractions, and make sure that what's behind you looks neat, modern and organized, even if the rest of your office is a mess. These subtleties will help you make a better, and more professional, first impression.

Watch the background noises when you're doing virtual calls. Dogs barking, babies crying and phones ringing are a distraction to what you're saying and hearing. Again, you won't get credit for getting it right, but they will notice those other noises and it does affect how they hear, and perceive what you're saying. I know that your kids are adorable, but they don't belong on your appointments. Same goes for your dog(s). Some of you are disagreeing with me right now, because you feel that it's endearing to share your family with your clients. You feel that it makes you a real person. That may be true for some couples, but to others it can signal a less than professional demeanor.

If you're meeting them in person take a look at your meeting space from their perspective. That's really hard to do because you have the *"Curse of Knowledge"* – you see it every day, so it's hard for you to see what they'll focus on. Try to have someone who's never been to your office tell you what they see. This isn't just about deferred maintenance items. Does the furniture and décor match your brand? If you're targeting a higher-end clientele, your offices need to reflect that. Your choice of clothing needs to reflect that. And yes, even your address needs to reflect that. The higher up the price scale you go, the more appearances matter. I wish it weren't true, but it is. If you're charging top dollar for your market, and they pull up and see a beat-up van in your driveway, they might leave without even coming in. When I was publishing the WeddingPages magazine for New Jersey, I had a mid-priced venue that placed an ad that looked very upscale. They told me that they saw Mercedes Benz cars pull up at their venue for appointments, and then turn around and drive off. The first impression didn't match the ad. Be the best at who you really are. Don't try to look like something you're not. If you want to move up higher on the price scale, do the heavy lifting first. Invest in the better website. Invest in better branding and design. Invest in your offices, vehicle (if applicable) and more. Invest in your success first, if you want others to invest in you!

Seeing the scene from their eyes is also about seeing the clutter, cobwebs, crooked photos on the wall, and any other distractions. If you're trying to sell a wedding couple, having photos of Bar Mitzvahs, Quinceañeras and/or corporate parties is a distraction. This couple wants to know that you're a wedding specialist. These days that's an easy fix. You can replace the wall photos with a flat screen TV. You can stream images that are relevant to them, and change those images for each audience. I've seen many DJs with flat screen TVs that have been adorned with picture frames, making them look classier, and less like technology. Get creative and make it part of your décor.

Apple, Google and others have devices that let you stream

anything from your smartphone or laptop to your TV, seamlessly, including music. If you have more than one space where you meet couples, you can have more than one of these units, and stream, or pull up different images as you walk the client around. Imagine it's winter time and gardens are bare, and you're able to pull up beautiful images of real weddings at their venue that show the cafe lighting you did on the outdoor patio. Sure, you can pull out a photo album. But it's much more dramatic to pull up the right photo, in the moment. This works great on an iPad or other tablet computer. You should be trying to close the sale when they are most emotionally connected to the end result of what you're going to do for them. Showing them an empty banquet room with lighting, or your DJ setup, isn't going to do that. Showing them people dancing at real weddings is much better. You don't need a special app for this, just use photo galleries (albums), which all smartphones and tablet computers have.

You can have different photo albums, categorized by venue, or color, or style, or ceremony/reception, or anything that makes sense for your business. If you want to take the time to tag your images with keywords or categories, a quick search will pull up the relevant images. It takes some prep time, but if you get in the habit of tagging them when you upload them to your device, it won't take much time at all.

While you're in an appointment, and I know this sounds obvious, don't take phone calls, check your smartphone, or email. It's rude and it shows them that they're less important than whatever else you're doing. When you're the customer you don't like that. So, unless someone close to you is about to have a baby, or coming out of surgery, silence your devices, and tell you staff (if you have a staff) not to interrupt you unless it relates to this customer. People believe what they see more than what they hear, and your actions speak volumes. Giving them your undivided attention is key to gaining their trust. I've said this already, but it's worth mentioning again - people buy from people they know, like and trust. Treat each customer and appointment separately. Let's see how you can learn to hit the reset button before each appointment.

CHAPTER 17

Hit the reset button

What happened in your last meeting has no bearing on the next one (unless you made the sale as I want that energy brought forward). The next customer's entertainment needs are different. Their history is different. Their goals are different. And, their expectations are different. It's only through asking better questions, and really listening to the answers, where we'll find out what we need to make this sale.

Hitting the reset button is hard. Your brain remembers that it just talked about this feature, or related this story, with the previous customer. So, you may omit certain things from the next conversation. I once had a DJ client hire me to sit in their office and watch him have real appointments, with real wedding clients. He had two meetings that day, each with a bride and her Mom, one in the morning, one in the afternoon. I noticed that in the afternoon appointment, he didn't say some of the same things he had said in the morning. Now, don't get me wrong, each appointment should be different, but if it's appropriate, some of the same things should get said. We don't realize that we're omitting those things, or we would say them. The key is to say the appropriate things to each customer in their appointment. You should try to close each sale when it's time, but never try to rush the sale. Some will take 5 minutes, some 55 minutes, some days or weeks. We'll discuss that more as we move forward.

Hitting the reset button is important before every phone call, email, in-person or virtual appointment. It's part of being present with the customer. Being present is learning to tune out everything else, and focusing on what you're doing now. In the sensory-overloaded world we live in, being present is really hard. Your attention is constantly being pulled in many directions, be it checking your email, getting texts, phones ringing (although many of you wish your customers would call more than emailing or texting), and the many other distractions we face, every day.

Being present is hard when it comes to your family and relationships, too. This isn't just a work phenomenon. There's an expression "the second screen", which refers to times when you're watching TV and also checking your smartphone (which is usually the 2nd screen). For many of us there's a 3rd or 4th screen, as well. Many believe this has led to our shorter attention spans.

I learned how to be more present when I was practicing Tae Kwon Do. Many of you have heard, or read stories of my journey to a 2nd degree Black Belt, starting when I was 39 years old. Tae Kwon Do has influenced many things in my life, and learning to be more present is one of the most important. In life, if you're not being present you might miss something someone said, or a body language cue. You might miss a scene of a movie or TV show. If you're not being present while practicing martial arts, you're likely getting kicked or hit. That doesn't have to happen too many times before you start to learn to be more present and in tune with what's happening around you.

One of the things I loved about going to Tae Kwon Do classes was that my mind would clear of everything else. I would only think about what we were doing, right now. It was a very spiritual experience because that's hard to do in our daily lives. We need to create those spaces so we can have the bandwidth to come up with new ideas, new perspectives and, to listen and pay attention to what's happening around us.

Have you ever come up with a great idea while in the shower? Yeah, I have too. Why is that? You're in a place where you can't easily write down that great idea, and you're afraid you'll forget it. The same goes for when you wake up in the middle of the night, and you've solved that business issue that's been eluding you. You're afraid you won't remember it in the morning. Part of the reason you get those ideas is that you're removed from the other distractions that have clouded your path to that answer. By not thinking about that question or problem for a while you've actually made it easier to see a different solution. Google and Amazon.com have solved both of those problems for me. AquaNotes® and NiteNote® are two great inventions that have helped me. I can now write down my ideas while in the shower, or in the middle of the night.

Another very important time to hit the reset button is for referrals. What you know with a referral is that they've heard at least enough good things to contact you. They may have personally experienced your DJ, lighting or photo booth services at a friend's wedding, or just gotten your name from someone. You don't know how many other DJ companies they've been referred to. You don't know if their budget is anything like what their friend spent with you. They may have an idea of what you charge, but often they're wrong, either because their friend's wedding was several years ago, or their friend didn't show them the contract. They told them what they remembered paying (which is often less than the final price because of tax, or service charge, or just because they are embarrassed by how much it really was). So, hitting the reset button is a simple as saying *"I'm so glad the Millers referred you to us. Their wedding was so much fun, and they were great to work with. Tell me how we can make your wedding everything you've imagined, and more."* And then stop talking, and really listen.

Can you tell when someone isn't giving you their full attention? I'm sure you can, even when you're on the phone. You can also tell in an email if someone is really replying to what you've written, or if they're not giving your email their full attention. Well, guess what? Your customers can tell, too. That's why hitting the reset button is so important. You need to clear the slate and really pay attention to each customer and their needs. They'll notice, and so will you when you make more sales.

CHAPTER 18

Your Marketing Materials Won't Close the Sale for You

Whether you've hired a professional graphic designer and/or copywriter to help you with your marketing materials, or you've done them yourself, don't expect them to close the sale for you. That's your job! Marketing materials can help with conversion. If they're projecting the right image and supporting your brand and image, they can help to convince people who didn't come in for the meeting (or weren't able to join you on the virtual meeting). I've found that marketing materials can also be a detriment when they don't accurately represent your brand. I've seen beautiful websites that have really bad collateral materials, in the form of PDFs, that bring down the brand image. Many have no design (because they're intended to be printed on your letterhead), too many fonts, or hard to read fonts (too scripty), too many colors, and way too much of the "what", without the "why hire *you*". All it would take is a small investment in a graphic designer to make them outstanding. When it comes to things like this you shouldn't focus on the cost. You should focus on the benefit.

Do you want to know what better graphic design costs? I answered this earlier in this book when referring to what a new website costs: it costs less than the business you lose by having poor, or no design. Can you tell when someone has made their marketing pieces themselves versus those done by a professional graphic designer? I'm sure you can, and so can your clients. Every one of our marketing pieces is professionally designed, and printed on high-quality paper. We're all being judged by whatever our prospects see.

When it comes to the printing, quality also matters here. I've tried using some of the discount printers, but the colors and quality are inconsistent. Instead we have a printer that we know we can trust, their turnaround is quick and the quality is consistent. We also have a real person to talk to, who's keeping an eye on our jobs. Does it cost a little more? We don't look at it that way. What would it cost us to lose even one sale by having inferior materials? Way more than the difference in the cost of printing. You want customers to hire you because you're the professionals, right? Then you, and I, should do the same.

One of the things our graphic designer created is a style guide. Professional designers use these, as do magazines and websites, to have consistency across a brand. The style guide specifies the fonts, colors, type sizes, even the paper stock and whether the corners are rounded. If I were to lay out all of your company's printed collateral materials on a table, would they all look as if they belong to the same company? Or, are you holding on to some of the older pieces, even though you have a newer, better design? Have you rebranded your DJ business and are waiting until you run out of the old business cards and marketing pieces, until you print new ones? You don't want to run out of customers before you run out of old collateral materials.

While it costs more per piece, we print only what we need for the short-term. It's tempting to go for doubling the order size for only a small increase in price, but I've found that almost every time we print something, when it arrives we like it, but already have an idea on how to improve them. It's very rare that we just ask the printer to duplicate an order with the same artwork. It's part of the process of constantly looking to improve in every area. It's good enough for today, just never as good as it can ever be.

If your business has multiple audiences, or multiple services, you should consider having specific pieces for each of them. Just as with websites, wedding couples don't need or want to see corporate photos, or bar/bat mitzvah images, or birthday videos. It's your job to reduce the distractions here, too, and keep them focused on what you can do for them. Again, it might cost more to print separate pieces, than one brochure that shows everything you do, but that targeting could end up bringing you more business, which makes the extra cost insignificant.

When looking at printing, or better design, always consider the potential return, not just the cost. The difference between expensive and inexpensive is not the cost. Something is expensive when it brings you little or no return on your investment (ROI). Something is inexpensive when it brings you a good ROI, regardless of what it cost. Are you willing to let poor design, or poor quality printing damage your brand image? It costs so little more to get it right. Be sure to invest in your business the way you want your customers to invest in you.

CHAPTER 19

Make it all about them, and assume the sale

Whether it's the wording in your emails to them, the text on your website and in your marketing, or what they hear you say in an appointment (virtual or in-person), make it all about them. They don't care what you've done (your DJ experience), unless you bring that around to why it should matter to them. How does it make you the better choice for them? Remember that you're selling outcomes, not processes, so talk about the outcome that they'll get by hiring you as their DJ.

They expect that you have good experience, and they've probably already read about it on your website. You don't go to a restaurant and expect bad food or bad service, do you? As I often say in my presentations and consulting, use aspirational text on your website and in your marketing. Don't talk about your DJ experience without talking about the aspirational outcome that they want. If you're getting the chance to have a conversation with them, assume that you can close that sale. Exude confidence in your language and attitude.

Speak to them as if they've already bought. Don't say *"If you choose us as your DJ..."*. Say *"When you choose us as your DJ..."*, *"When your guests arrive..."*, *"When we discuss your introduction (first dance, ceremony, etc.)."* This is part of assuming the sale, which is very important. I wrote earlier about the many buying signals that have happened before you get to connect with them. I also mentioned about how many other DJs or lighting companies, in your market, will never hear from them, and never even know they're shopping for your services. If you're having a conversation with them, I think you should proceed as if you know they're going to buy from you. It's your sale to win or lose. You should speak to them as if they're going to buy from you. Confidence is attractive in business relationships as well as personal ones. Confidence sells.

Start listening to your language, whether written or oral. See if you're talking about them, and the outcomes they'll get, or if you're talking about what you do. Just as with your website and marketing, using the words "you", and "your" is critical to closing more sales. Use visual expressions. Paint mental pictures for them and be sure to put them in the picture by talking to them about their outcomes. When they can start to "see" what you're going to do for them, and are picturing specifically you providing that outcome, it becomes harder to choose someone else. Use stories and analogies when doing sales presentations. People will remember the meaning of the stories, even if they don't remember the details. I've had people relate to me a story they said they heard from me, but I didn't recall telling it. Their story had the same, or similar meaning to one I had told, but they had put their own spin on it. Stories and mental pictures stick in our memories better than words alone. It's also easier to get them to picture the outcome of doing business with you when you use aspirational words and pictures.

Assuming the sale is also key to closing the sale, especially on the first appointment, or in the first meeting. If you're getting the chance to meet with them, it's because they want and/or need a DJ, lighting and/or photo booth. If you believe you can close the sale on the first appointment, you'll have a better chance of doing so. It's the same at wedding shows. If you believe you can make sales at the wedding show, then you have a much better chance of doing so.

I know of a wedding show promoter who has proven to his exhibitors that they can make sales at his shows. He pays the first 10 exhibitors who bring him signed contracts with deposits, 10% of the deposit amount, up to $250 each. He's willing to invest up to $2,500 of his own money to prove that it works. You better believe that his exhibitors are much more likely to try to make sales, knowing that they'll get that money. They come prepared with contracts and a way to take a deposit. Do you? It's not luck, it's preparation and confidence. The Roman philosopher Seneca said, **"Luck happens when preparation meets opportunity."**

CHAPTER 20

Don't have a sales pitch, just talk to them

Many of you have a well-rehearsed sales pitch. Every appointment, starts out the same way, and you're very comfortable talking about all of the great things you're going to do for that couple. Contrary to that, we like to tell every couple, company or customer that they're unique. Well, if they're so unique, why are you doing the same sales pitch, every time? Remember the title of this book, *"Shut Up and Sell More"*. They key is talking less, and selling more.

When I'm giving a presentation, whether there are 20 people in the room, or 2,000, everything I say on stage, I already know. While I might phrase some parts differently each time, the underlying content is all mine, so I already know it. However, I come up with my new topic ideas by listening, not talking. I listen to the questions that I'm asked. I listen to the conversations that DJs are having in person, online and those that I'm emailed. I listen to patterns to show me what's important to you, my audience.

Since every wedding, every couple, every bar/bat mitzvah and every corporate event really is unique, the only way we're going to find out how to make the sale is by listening. Like me, if you're talking, you're only going to hear things you already know. If you ask them better questions, and you're really listening to their answers, you'll hear everything you need to know to make that sale. That's why having a "sales pitch" can get in the way. You're going through your pitch (talking), instead of giving them a chance to tell you what's important to them (listening), what they've already seen, and even what you should avoid talking about. Remember the phrase *"selling yourself right out of the sale"*. This refers to when you keep talking when the customer is ready to buy. If you talk too much they start to lose interest, because you missed the buying signals. That means that they're feeling like you're not as connected to their needs as you should be.

I mentioned earlier about the DJ who had me sit in on two, actual wedding appointments. Each was with a bride and her mom, one in the morning, and one in the afternoon. This particular DJ has a well-rehearsed sales pitch. It's smooth and polished. The problem is that it doesn't leave room for questions. It's a lot of talking, not a lot of asking. While there were parts that I liked, for the most part it felt too scripted. The other problem was that he was somewhat disconnected, and he missed some key buying signals, because he was chugging along with his pitch, like a train on rails. Trains on rails can't zig or zag around obstacles. They have to keep chugging straight on their path. But sales appointments aren't straight lines. They're going to jump around based upon the questions you ask, and more importantly, the answers you get.

This applies to all kinds of sales appointments, regardless of what you're selling. Back when I was publishing two wedding magazines, I had hired a young lady to do sales. She didn't have a lot of sales experience, so I was trying to teach her to ask better questions. She asked me what some better questions were, and wrote them down. A couple of weeks later she came to me and said that she didn't think the questioning was working. I soon realized why. She had typed out all of the questions and had them printed as forms on a clip board. It turns out she was asking every customer, every question. She had totally missed the point. Making more sales wasn't about asking every customer, every question. It was about asking one good question, really listening to their answer, and then deciding what to talk about next.

For instance, instead of telling them about your uplighting, ask them *"Have you thought about how uplighting can extend your color scheme throughout your banquet room?"* If they say "Yes", and tell you how much they love the effect, then you can tell them more about what you can do for them. However, if you ask them about uplighting (monogram, dancing in the clouds, or any of your options) and they tell you how they hate it, or have thought about it but don't want it, would you still "pitch" them on that feature? I hope not. But that's exactly what you're doing when your sales pitch includes those features, before you've asked if they want them, or are interested in hearing more. What is it that you're talking about, that your customers may not want, or need, to hear? Telling, without asking, is like walking into a minefield. You want to know where the mines are before you step in. Let's look at more ideas for better questions you can use.

CHAPTER 21

Asking better questions

Throughout the sales cycle you're building rapport with the couple or client. You do that through asking better questions, really listening to their answers, and then formulating what to ask, or say, next. If you haven't already gotten my many clues about this, making more sales is about asking better questions, throughout the process. But what's a better question? You can't, as my sales rep found out, just ask the same questions to every customer. You can have an opening question, but then you need to let the process ebb and flow with each couple. Some appointments will take minutes, some hours. Some will close today and some in days or weeks. Just accept that each is going to be different.

What questions are you asking your couples and other customers, that don't really give you any information you can use to make the sale? Yes or No questions are usually not as good as open-ended ones. All you get is a Yes or a No. That's fine if the question is, *"Are you ready to book our services?"* But, if you ask *"Do you want a photo booth?"*, getting a Yes, or No, doesn't give you any indication as to "why", just "what". If there's anything you've heard me hammering home, it's that they buy, and pay your price, because of the "why", not the "what". Your "what" looks the same on paper as every other DJ or entertainer.

Many of you ask polite, chit-chat questions, such as, *"Where did you meet?"* That's nice, and you can still ask it, but will that information help you learn anything about what they want for their wedding? Here are some examples of better, open-ended questions:

- Instead of asking *"Do you want a photo booth?"*, try asking *"Have you thought about something fun for your guests to do when they're not dancing?"* You'll get them thinking about the experience, rather than the service.

- Instead of asking which songs they want, try asking, *"Which song comes on that makes you quickly look at each other and smile?"* And then ask them the significance of that song.

- *"Which photo or video did you see on our website that had you look at each other, and you both just knew that you wanted to contact us?"* Then, as they're smiling in front of you thinking about it, ask them what it was about that photo or video that touched them.

- One of my favorite questions for you to ask gets them thinking about the success of their wedding. Ask them, *"On the Monday after your wedding, when your guests go back to work, and their co-workers ask them about it, what do you want them to say?"* Another way to phrase it is, *"If you could write your guest's review of your wedding, what would it say?"* Questions like this get them thinking about the outcomes they want. They also give you, if you're really listening, important words and phrases to take note of. You can repeat them when you're talking about what you're going to do for them. Words and phrases that come up, over and over, give you a clue as to their priorities.

What about Yes or No questions? Yes or No questions can be asked when the answer doesn't matter, or won't stop you from moving forward. For instance, if I'm speaking to someone about my website review services, I could ask, *"Do you have a website?"* Now, I'm pretty sure the answer is Yes. But, if the answer is No, they probably need my help, more-so than someone with a website.

Here are some other examples of Yes or No questions:

- If you're selling wedding entertainment you could smile and ask a Yes or No question to which you already know the answer, *"Are you looking for an experience that leaves your guests amazed?"* – this is an example of asking a question to which you already know the answer. You ask questions like this to get agreement from them, since you already know how they'll answer. You would then follow that with, *"Which parts of the experience we'll created together do you think will do that?"*

• You might ask, *"Do you have a do not-play list?"*, because you know they probably do. But again, that doesn't give you the why, just the what. Instead you might ask, *"Are there any things that you've seen at a wedding, that you absolutely don't want to have at yours, and why?"* (notice how to assume the sale).

• You can ask a variation of, *"Have you already decided to have your wedding here?"* no matter what you do (thanks to the late Mike Roman, founder of the catersource conference, for that one). Here are some examples, *"Have you already decided to have us DJ your wedding?"* and *"Have you already decided to have us bring the photo booth to your wedding?"* Say it with a smile, and not the very first question. If in your prior communications you've been hearing and reading buying signals (*"How much is the deposit?"*, *"When do we get to choose the____?"*), then you can, with confidence, assume the sale and go for the close.

• At a certain point in your conversation or meeting, when you're sensing good buying signals, you can ask *"Would it make sense to reserve your date now?"* I heard a fellow speaker suggest this and it's one of my new, favorite questions. What I love about this is that it puts the decision back onto your customer, but in a very low-pressure way. I've used this, and it's likely that you've already used this, we just hadn't thought of it as a "technique"… that is, until now. Variations would be, *"Would it make sense to select your monogram style now?"* or, *"Would it make sense to choose your first dance song now?"* or for a multi-op *"Would it make sense to choose your DJ now?"* Remember, you're actually not trying to sell them. You're trying to help them buy.

CHAPTER 22

Help Them Buy

Why do your appointments take longer than they should? In a word: You! You want to talk more than listen, tell more than ask and present more than have a conversation. You won't really listen to the meaning of their answers. It's time to stop talking, so you can sell more. If you've ever found yourself thinking about the next thing you want to say, while the other person is talking, you're not really listening. As I've said, given the chance, every customer will tell you exactly what they want to buy. But, that means you have to give them a chance. You don't know what they're going to say when you ask a question. Have you ever been surprised by something someone wants? I'm sure you have. There's been a trend towards personalization in weddings for years. That means listening is even more important than ever, so you can hear when they tell you what they want.

No one likes to be "sold". Being sold implies that it was the salesperson's idea of what you should buy. Yes, they need your guidance, especially for weddings where they've probably never reserved a DJ, MC, lighting or a photo booth before. However, guidance isn't the same as deciding what they want and need. Buyer's remorse is when you second guess your purchase decision, after the fact. This happens when you don't feel confident about what you bought, and/or what you paid. That's a value judgment, not a price judgment.

Value has many more components than just price. If they don't believe that you can, and will, deliver as promised, then price doesn't matter. If they don't like their salesperson, then price doesn't matter. If they feel that they can get just as much value from another business, at a lower price, then they'll buy from that other business. People tend to buy from people they know, like and trust. They'll get to know you through better questioning and conversation. Asking them more questions that get them talking about what they want, makes them know, like and trust you more. Salespeople that don't seem to care about what their couples/customers want will not get that connection.

The key here is to stop selling and help them buy. When they feel it was their decision, they'll have less buyer's remorse. When you help them buy, they'll like you better because they see you as their partner and advocate, not as a "salesperson." To help them buy you need to find out their priorities, because that's where their money will go. The things that they value the most will get more of their budget. Have you ever seen a wedding where some things seemed to be out of proportion to their budget, either high, or low? Maybe a bride was wearing a very expensive dress, but they chose an off-season date to save on the venue? Or they chose the top catering package, but the DJ was lower-priced? Those decisions are about priorities, not price.

How do you know what they value the most? Ask them. I did a sales training for a group of affiliated catering venues. The discussion of asking the couple what they want was one of the key points for them. While they are already having success, they were using a sales pitch, touring the couples around their venue, and hitting on the highlights. Scripts are fine for training and reference, but not for selling. Theirs was a very polished pitch, but a pitch all the same. One of their salespeople emailed me a couple of days after our training to relate how changing her approach was working. A couple came in and she asked them what the most important things were about choosing their wedding venue. The bride said it was the photo locations and she wanted a Viennese dessert table (a very elaborate display and selection). The groom said that price was the most important factor for him, an indication that he was probably not as tuned in to the other decisions. I would have been watching to see if he was paying attention during the tour, and if he was asking any questions. Was he using words like *"It's her wedding"*, deferring to her for answers, or giving any other indications that he wasn't as involved? At the end of the appointment the bride said to the salesperson *"You're the only one who has asked us what we want."* She noticed it, and it was notable enough for her to verbalize. And yes, the salesperson made the sale.

What are you doing to be memorable? How are you getting them to remember you, and your company, especially after they've shopped around? Are you helping them buy, or selling? I once did a 10-minute WedTalk titled *"The Quick Close"*. The one, main point was to help them buy. It was about asking better questions, reducing the distractions, watching their body language and not being afraid to ask closing questions at any point in the discussion. These are all things I've been discussing in this book, only in greater detail (it's tough to get into detail with a 10-minute presentation). If you're having a good conversation or appointment, they're likely to bring up some objections. Let's see how to handle them so you can make more sales.

CHAPTER 23

Objections overruled!

One of the most misunderstood parts of the sales process is objections. Those of you who are not natural sales people hate objections. You see them as road blocks to getting the sale. I'm here to show you how to see them differently. In a perfect world of butterflies and rainbows, customers, couples and companies come to you, love everything you do, and open their wallets without any resistance. Of course in the real world you have competition, many of whom also do a very good job, have great reviews, and yes, sometimes have lower prices for similar services. During the sales process you're going to be confronted with objections, some big, some small, that often delay or derail the sale. Some are genuine and some are just their way of saying, *"We don't want to hire you as our DJ"*, *"We need more convincing about your DJ/MC services"* and/or simply: *"We want to leave."* Helping them buy, instead of selling them, can help reduce these objections.

There's a big difference between order-taking and selling. Order-taking is when the customer comes to you, tells you what they want, and then they buy it for the price you're asking. That's what happens at many retail stores and fast food restaurants. The selling starts when you ask the first question - *"Do you want fries with that?"* - or hear the first objection, which is often a question - *"Do we have to stick to that package?"* or *"Is that the only DJ you have for our date?"*. Not asking them any questions will cost you lots of money in lost sales. I'll be discussing the concept of **"Opportunity Cost"** in a later chapter, but suffice it to say here that, for many of you, the difference between your DJ or lighting business surviving and thriving, often comes down to the opportunity cost of not asking for the bigger sale.

What is an objection? It's when your customer brings up something, whether you've already discussed it yet or not, that adds a "but" into the conversation. In other words *"We would buy from you, but..."*. To many novice sales people, or wedding pros who've been reluctantly selling, but don't really like the selling part of their work, objections are a hassle. It would be so much easier if they'd just buy your DJ services or reserve your photo booth without any objections. Once again, this is the real world and your customers can, and will object. Unless you're selling a commodity, something they can buy "off the shelf" (without needing your assistance), there will be objections, or at least questions.

Most objections are speed bumps that slow down the sale, not road blocks that stop it. Speed-bump objections are usually just questions. Here are some examples:

- *"Do the monograms come in any other colors?"*

- *"Can we customize the items in the package?"* (if the answer is No, they may still buy)

- *"Can we talk about our song choices before we do the contract?"* (is this a necessity or just a desire?)

- *"Can you do better on the price?"* (yes, that's a speed bump, not a road block, a bit more on that later).

Road-block objections are things that are harder, or impossible to overcome, such as when you're not available on their date, or can't meet their deadline… or they don't like or trust that you'll be able to deliver. I said a few times already, but it bears repeating - people buy from people they know, like and trust. No matter how much they like your work, if they don't like you, they'll find someone else, even if it means spending more. People buy your value, not your price, and part of that value proposition are the intangibles associated with the buying process. The intangibles include your response time, how easy, or hard you make it to do business with you, and how excited you are about their wedding (it may be your 500th, but it's their first, or at least they want it to be their last). If you ask them better questions and really listen to the answers (which is the main theme of this book), they'll like you better. The more they're talking, the more you're learning about them, and their needs, and what it will take to make the sale.

Letting them voice objections is part of the process. As a matter of fact, here's a great sale-closing question, *"Is there any reason we shouldn't move forward with reserving us for your wedding?"* If they say "No" then write up the sale. If they say "Yes", and you give them a chance to tell you what those reasons are - and really listen - you'll find out some very important information. They're about to tell you why they haven't yet bought. Objections are good, as they give you a window into why they haven't yet signed up (assuming you've been asking for the sale – read on for more on that). Objections give them the chance to feel that they're special, and that they're getting something that's not one-size-fits-all for their wedding. Therefore, contrary to what you might have thought, you actually want your customers to object. If they're not making any objections, and they're not yet buying, what's missing? You're probably not asking for the sale.

Objections are opportunities to show them your expertise. Objections are opportunities to show them that you're really listening. I know, you'd rather have it the easy way, but if everyone is just saying "Yes" without any objections, your prices are probably way too low. Your goal is to fill your calendar with the people you want to work with, based upon their style, vision, personality and budget. Everyone who inquires can't fit that list. A bridezilla or groomzilla, with a really high budget, is still probably a sale you don't want. A really nice couple, with a really low budget, isn't the way to fill a Saturday night in wedding season either. If you know you can fill that date at a higher package and price, you have the right to hold out for someone who's spending more. That's why many entertainment companies have revenue minimums for certain dates. If you a DJ, you don't have to offer your lowest package on a popular date. You can set your own minimum revenue requirement for those dates as well. This is especially true for single-ops, where your inventory is one - you!

Objections are buying signals. Most people don't negotiate for things they don't want. If they weren't interested, they wouldn't bother asking the question, or voice the objection. When they say *"what if…"* or *"but…"*, they're really saying *"I'll be closer to buying if you answer this well."* It's really just a mindset shift to see these as opportunities. If they weren't interested, you never would have gotten the inquiry, no less the meeting. If they aren't still interested they would either stop replying, hang up or leave – if you're meeting with them in person.

Even price objections are buying signals. They're signaling that if you can show them the value, or another option, they might buy. Again, if they weren't interested at all, the sales process would just stop. But it isn't stopping, they're hanging in there with you. I'm not saying you need to lower your price to get the sale. I've done many webinars and live presentations about value, so please don't lower your price without getting something of value back in return, something we'll cover a little later.

Don't create your own objections. I was speaking at an event in Mexico and a DJ who was attending told me that he never works at the hotel where the conference was being held, because they charge $500 for someone to bring in a DJ who's not on their preferred list. I told him that it wasn't his decision, it was the customer's decision. If they really want him for thier wedding, add the $500 to his rate. By assuming that the customer won't pay the extra $500 he's cutting off the possibility of working at that hotel. He doesn't know if the customer will object unless he quotes the price. He has nothing to lose and everything to gain.

CHAPTER 24

Handling specific objections

I don't like using the word "techniques" when teaching sales. The word implies a level of manipulation, which is counter to helping people buy. I want people to buy from you because they feel you're the best choice, the best value and because you want them as customers. That said, you need to know how to address their questions and objections, to keep the sales process moving forward, getting you all closer to the sale. When I was VP of Sales at The Knot, my sales team dubbed me *"The Objections Guy"*, because there wasn't an objection they could bring me, that I couldn't help them resolve. I showed them that you can't change someone's mind, but you can provide them with information they didn't already have, which may help them come to a different conclusion. We all see things through our own eyes and history, and make decisions based upon what we already know. When we get new information, it can either confirm what we know, or give us a new perspective which can lead us to a different conclusion.

Here are some tools (not techniques) to help you address common objections:

Agree when they disagree

One of the best ways to diffuse an objection is to agree with them. If you've tried to close the sale and couldn't, and they say, "*We want to go home and think about it.*" You can say "*Of course you do. I wouldn't expect you to make such an important decision at our first meeting.*" However, if you hear this often: "*You've given us so much to think about, we need to go home and process it.*", and that's why you don't close many sales on the first appointment... that's your fault, not theirs. It's called Decision-Paralysis, the inability to make a decision when presented with too many choices. Your job is to help reduce their choices down to only the most appropriate for their wedding or event, not confuse them with every lighting or special-effect item you offer. No one needs everything you offer. So, don't show them every song, style of gobo, photo strip design or lighting choice. That is information overload. Listen first to the outcome they want, then show them how you can get them to that, or a better outcome.

Feel – Felt – Found

One of the best ways to handle most objections is with a process that I heard many, many years ago. I've tried to find the origin of it, but even Google can't help me. It's so simple, yet so effective. There are 3 parts to this:

- **Feel** – empathize with their situation

- **Felt** – show them that others, just like them, have had this same thought
- **Found** – is what you wanted to say to overcome the objection, but doing that right away would be more confrontational.

Here's how this works with real objections (hint – it works really well):

Objection *"You're the first DJ we've seen. We need to look around."*

Response *"I understand how you feel. Many other couples we've seen have felt that they need to do an endless DJ search. What they have found is that they, like you, have already done a lot of the research online, and you know what you want before you get here. So once you find it, you reserve it, even if it's the first company you've visited. Why keep looking when your must-have list is covered? And that's why so many couples reserve us for their weddings on their first appointment. Should we go ahead and reserve your date?"*

Objection *"That's more than we want to spend on a DJ."*

Response *"I totally understand how you feel and I know how things add up for weddings. I had a couple in last week who felt the same way. They found that,*

> when it comes to their wedding DJ, there were things they hadn't thought of when they made their budget, and there are other places they can try to save. And so, they went with us because they didn't want to look back after their wedding and have their guests think they skimped on their entertainment. Should we go ahead and reserve your date?"

There are countless ways to use Feel – Felt – Found, even if you don't use those exact words. I want to give you a foundation for coming up with your own wording, phrasing you'll feel comfortable using in real sales appointments. Play around with this and you'll find that it's almost magical how well it works. It's a much softer, more comfortable process for both you, and your couples. Here's an example using alternative wording:

> **Objection** *"That's too much money for a photo booth."*

> **Response** *"If price is the most important factor when choosing your photo booth, then we're not going to be the right choice. Couples like you don't choose us because you want the lowest price. You choose us because you want your guests raving about the experience long after your wedding. Should we go ahead and reserve this booth for you?"*

When they come back

When your customers go looking around, and come back to you and say *"We found a lower price with another DJ."* – what they're really saying is *"We want to book with you, but this lower price is making us confused."* Think about it, if they had found everything they want, and need, including a lower price, why didn't they book that other company? It's because they really want you to do their wedding. You don't have to match the price to get the sale. You have to remind them of the value of choosing you, over anyone else. Try a response like this: *"I'm sure the other DJ company does a good job for what they're charging. If they could give you the results you that we can, surely they'd be charging what we do, maybe more!"* Of course, you can certainly use Feel – Felt – Found here: *"I understand how you feel, and thanks for coming back. I had a couple in the other day who had also looked around and got a lower price from another DJ. What they found was a lower price is easy to find, but it's not the price that will make your wedding great. It's our creative, dedicated people, working tirelessly for you, before and during your wedding that make the difference, and that's why they went with us. Should we reserve your date now?"*

Once you're comfortable handling objections you still need to ask for the sale. Let's see ways you can get better at that.

CHAPTER 25

Asking for the sale

Probably the easiest way to close more sales is to start asking for the sale. I know that sounds obvious, but the reason you're not closing more sales is because you've either missed the buying signals, or you're waiting for them to say, "*Let's do this. Write up the order!*" Oh, sure, that happens once in a blue moon. In sales lingo it's called a "lay-down". In the real world you have to ask for the sale, and you have to ask for it early and often. You close the sale when they're ready to buy, not at a particular point in the sales pitch (because, as I said earlier, you shouldn't have a sales pitch). The end of the appointment is always at the close; but the close isn't always at the same point. That's why many of your appointments are taking longer than they should. You're not asking for the sale earlier.

After I presented a webinar on closing the sale, a wedding cake baker wrote to me with a story. The day after the webinar a couple came in to her shop for their appointment. As she was talking with them, she was noting their preferences on an order form, as she had done with other couples. Only this time she looked down at the order form, early in the appointment, and it had all of the details she needed to make their cake. In the past she would have continued the "pitch" about her products and services for at least another 30 minutes. Instead, a little voice inside her head (one that sounded just like me) told her to stop selling. She turned the order form around so the couple could see it, and she reviewed the details with them. She then asked, *"Did I get this right? Do I have everything you want me to do for your wedding cake?"* And then she "shut up" and waited for them to answer. They looked at each other, then at her, and said, *"Yes"*. So the little voice in her head said, *"Ask for the money!"* So, she asked them, *"How did you want to leave the deposit - cash, check or credit card?"* They took out their credit card, she ran the deposit, they signed the order and credit card slip, and they left. After they were out of her shop, she told me that she wanted to explode. She hadn't told them half of the things she normally says in a consultation. Right. They bought without having to hear all of those other things. That's the point of listening and watching for the buying signals.

I want to give you a few different ways to ask for the sale. Again, I don't call them "techniques" because that can have a negative implication, as if you're somehow cheating or tricking them into buying. Nothing could be further from my intention. I want them to buy from you because you're the right fit. I want them to buy from you because you want to be their wedding or event DJ/MC, you want to do their lighting or photo booth, because you will enjoy having them as customers, and because they're paying you a fair price for the value you're providing. You don't want to close every sale. If you've been in business longer than a year, you know that there are some customers you just don't want. I was sitting at dinner at a conference with an event decorator who's been in the business for over 20 years. He said that there are some customers that you just can't satisfy. Their vision for the wedding is an unrealistic fairytale, often fueled by Pinterest and Instagram, that their budget just doesn't support (don't you wish those photos came with price tags?). Your goal is to exceed their expectations. You have to choose to work with people with whom that's achievable.

OK, back to closing the sale. Here are a few tools to help you close more of the people with whom you get to have a conversation:

1) Just ask for the sale: I know this sounds obvious, but if you want the sale, ask for the sale. When you get a buying signal, or overcome an objection, regardless of where you are in the appointment, your next question should be asking for the sale:

- *"We can absolutely have the lighting for you in that color, should I get that reserved for you now?"*

- *"Yes, this DJ is available for your date, shall I reserve her for you now?"*

- "Which package have you decided to go with?"
- "What would you like to happen next?"
- "Is there any reason we shouldn't move forward with reserving this photo booth for your date?"
- "I'm ready to start planning your amazing wedding... entertainment now, are you?"

Don't overcomplicate things. Asking for the sale is a natural next step. Here's how it looks after you overcome an objection. You'll remember this from an earlier chapter. Adding that one question, after you've used feel-felt-found, changes it from a statement, to a close:

Objection *"You're the first DJ we've seen. We need to look around."*

Response *"I understand how you feel. Many other couples we've seen have felt that they need to do an endless DJ search. What they found is that they, like you, have already done a lot of the research online, and you know what you want before you get here. So once you find it, you buy it, even if it's the first company you've seen. Why keep looking when your must-have-for-entertainment list is covered? And that's why so many buy from us on their first appointment. Should we reserve Chris for your wedding now?"*

2) Ask a variation of "Have you already decided to have your wedding here?" Mike Roman, who founded the catersource conference, taught that if you know they've been to your venue for a friend or relative's wedding, or have some other strong connection to you, then go ahead and ask this question, early in the appointment. If they say *"Yes"*, then don't take them on a tour, or go through a lengthy meeting. Stop selling when they're already sold! Ask them *"So, did you have any specific questions, or shall we reserve your date?"* Now, some of you are thinking, sure, that might work for a venue, but not for a DJ. Why not? If you're a DJ, you too can say, *"Have you already decided to have us bring an amazing, creative experience to your wedding?"*

3) The choice or alternative close: This is one of those closing tools that you've already been using, you just don't realize it. When your customer has whittled their selection down to two options (DJs, photo booths, packages, etc.), you can simply ask *"So, did you want to go with option A, or option B?"* And then... *"shut up"* and wait for an answer. If they say either option A or option B, it's a sale. Then say, *"Terrific, let's get that reserved for you."*, and write up the sale. Again, don't overcomplicate it. Your job is not to confuse them with all of the options. Your job is to help narrow them down so they can make a decision to choose your company. If they've come down to only one option, then say, *"It sounds like you want to go with option C, shall I reserve that for your wedding?"* Then *"shut up"* and wait for an answer. If they say *"Yes"*, don't talk, just write it up.

If you have more than 2 or 3 choices, it's your job to avoid confusing them and make it easier for them to decide. Before showing them all of your options, have a conversation to figure out which of your choices will, and will not work for them (DJs, packages, lighting, photo booths, etc.). Then, only show them the options that will best fit their needs, preferably only 1 or 2 choices.

The choice close also works for when you're setting an appointment or scheduling a call. Instead of asking them *"What's a good day/time for you?"*, give them two options. The choices can be *"Morning or afternoon?"*, *"Tuesday or Thursday?"*, or more specifically *"Tuesday at 10 a.m. or Thursday at 2 p.m.?"* If neither of the choices works for them, they can always reply with another day or time. In any case, you'll be getting to a decision a lot faster than if you leave it open. Additionally, when you suggest specific days and times, it makes you appear busier, and therefore more in demand.

The key to closing the sale is asking for the sale. They're not going to tell you to write it up, it's your job to ask. And, you need to do so earlier in the conversation, or appointment, than you have been. Get confirmation along the way that you're on the right track. During the meeting (in-person or virtual), confirm details, large and small, so they know you're listening, and they start feeling like you're the right choice. Whether it's regarding timing, music, colors, or theme, repeating back to them the details lets you both know that you're moving forward. Asking for the sale along the way is called "trial closes". After confirming a detail, you use a closing question, such as *"Great, I'm glad we have the details, shall we go ahead and reserve us for your date?"* If they're not ready, they'll tell you. If they say, *"No, not yet"*, you can just say *"No worries, let's keep working on the details. I was just getting excited about your ideas and got ahead of myself."*

Now that you know more about how to ask for the sale, let's look at when you should ask.

CHAPTER 26

When to ask for the sale

If you haven't already noticed, there's no specific time to ask for the sale with every couple/client. You ask for the sale when they've heard enough to buy, and when you're reading, hearing and/or seeing the buying signals (asking about details, payment terms, negotiating price, etc.). Whether it's 5 minutes into an appointment, 2nd meeting, or on their 3rd email, don't be afraid to ask for the sale. The old sales mantra, *"ABC – Always Be Closing"* is absolutely correct. If you're getting the chance to have a conversation with them, be it in person, on the phone, Zoom or through email (or some other digital medium), you should always be closing.

I've heard from many wedding and event pros that they never ask for the sale on the first appointment. When I hear this, the sales trainer in me starts to twitch, as it signals to me that they're losing sales. Customers who were ready to buy were sent on their merry way, only to meet with some other DJ who booked them. Don't impart your own buying style on your customers. Just because you wouldn't buy on the first appointment, doesn't mean this couple won't. I was consulting with a venue who told me that she tells all of her couples to go home and think about it, and then get back to her with their decision. I nearly fell off my chair! If they didn't say, *"We want to think about it"*, why would you tell them to think about it? Then, she told me about a couple who came in, really liked her venue, and she told them to go home and think about it. They got halfway down her driveway and stopped, turned around and came back and told her, *"We don't need to think about it, we want to have our wedding here!"* This should have proven to her that not everyone needs to go home and think about it. If you're wondering, *"Should I try to close them on the first appointment?"*, my answer is unequivocally, **YES!** As I said earlier, if you've never closed anyone on the first appointment, it's not their fault, it's yours for not asking. As I'm writing this special edition, my good friend's son is engaged. They did their online research but only visited the one venue they really wanted. Sure, they looked at more online, but only visited the one, and booked it on the first appointment. The bride also bought the dress she saw in the shop window... on the first appointment. And they had a call with a videographer I recommended and, yup, booked him on the first call. Not everyone buys the same way, or the way you would.

Watch for buyer's fatigue – when they've been presented with so many creative ideas, or they've visited with so many different DJs, or they've look at so many videos, photos or samples, that their heads are spinning. They just want to be able to make a decision and move on to the next decision. When someone comes to you and you sense that they're on overload, bring that up and be the solution. Ask them, *"Are* your heads spinning from all of the choices you've seen? Are you starting to confuse each of the DJs with one another? Let me help make this easy for you. What have you seen that you absolutely have to have for your wedding entertainment, whether it's with us, or someone else? What do you know you don't want? Let me see if I can put something together that gives you everything you want, nothing you don't want, and then you can move forward with your other wedding decisions. How does that sound?" Buyer's fatigue can work in your favor. If they walk in with that deer-in-headlights look, help them by not confusing them with more and more choices. Simplify the process for them. If someone had already done that, you might not be meeting with them at all. Reduce the friction and be the easier solution.

Another question I've been asked is, *"Should I offer them an incentive to close on the first appointment?"* As with any other discounting or negotiating questions, this is a business decision that you have to make. I've done sales training for a bridal shop who offers a 10% discount if you buy on your first appointment. If you come back for a second appointment, the gowns are full price. If you want to come back for a 3rd appointment, you have to pay an appointment fee, and it doesn't go towards your purchase. They're placing a value on their consultants' time. Every time someone comes in for a second or third appointment, they're taking a time slot that could be used for a new prospect. What's your time worth? If you spend a lot of time doing appointments, then you may want to incentify them to buy on the first visit.

You can even explain to them that since you do a lot of work out of the view of your couples (music planning and editing, programming lighting, photo strip design, timelines, etc.), you want to maximize that time, so you offer an incentive if they choose you on that first visit. Personally, I wouldn't make it a discount, but rather an added value incentive: if you buy today, you'll get this extra product/service. When you discount your price, without taking anything away, you're giving away profit, not cost. If you didn't take away any services, they're going to cost you the same to deliver, but at a lower dollar amount. The difference is profit lost. When you give added services or products, you place a dollar value on them, but the actual cost of delivering them is lower. Giving them $500 off costs you $500 in profit, but giving them $500 in added lighting or décor costs you a fraction of that amount.

The same applies when you do a wedding show, or direct marketing campaign (email or postal mail). Offering an incentive of added value services or products can let you offer them a much higher dollar value, compared to the cost. If you're only offering a discount, you're always giving away profit, so be sure that your pricing structure supports that reduction. Ideally, if they want you and your team to be their DJ/MC, or to have you do their lighting or photo booth, you shouldn't have to make them an offer to close the sale. In the real world, some people are looking for an incentive, to make them feel better about their decision.

CHAPTER 27

Discounting versus Negotiating

For me, there's a big difference between discounting and negotiating. Discounting has a structure and rules. Negotiating is like the Wild West - no structure, no rules. The problem with negotiating is that you have to remember what you offered, and to whom. Also, in this digitally connected world, people talk and write about their experiences. If you're known as a negotiator, you're going to end up giving away more profit than necessary to close some sales. Whether it's their DJ, lighting or photo booth, every customer wants to know two things: that they got the very best price and that the next customer can't come along and get a better price. The best way to accomplish both of those is to charge everyone who buys the same services, the same pricing.

With discounting, a customer can get a lower price, but only if the rules apply to that situation. For instance, you may have a volume discount (based upon the number of events they do or how much they spend), and anyone who reaches that volume threshold qualifies for that discount. Or, you may have a package that includes a group of services or products, and the net cost of that package to them is lower than the individual pricing. That's a very common scenario, not just in the wedding and event industry, but in retail in general. I'll speak more about packages in the next chapter.

Having a discounting structure actually empowers your sales team, rather than restricting it. Knowing that you can't give a bigger discount allows you to say, with confidence, *"I appreciate you asking, but for this package, this lighting and this photo booth, that's the best price. Would you like to reserve those for your wedding? Or, if you'd like to look at a lower package, we can come up with something less expensive for you."* Never be offended by someone asking for a lower price. Some wedding pros, especially at the higher price points, have told me that they're offended when someone tries to negotiate with them. They can't believe that someone would try to get a lower price on their products and services. If you've ever asked anyone for a lower price on anything, you're a hypocrite for being offended when they ask you. You have the right to ask for a lower price, and so do they. You, the business, don't have to say yes. I'm sure you don't get a lower price every time you ask for one, either.

If you do decide to give them a discount, always get something in return. If you're the only one giving, then they're going to keep taking. It doesn't have to be something of equal value. Sometimes you just want to have them make a token gesture, just so that you've gotten something back. The value you get back might be a reduction in lighting services or time, a different photo booth, maybe a higher deposit, or even payment in full that day. Make them your partner in the negotiation, so it's a two-way street. Every time you give them something, get something back. They'll be sure to stop asking when they want to stop giving.

Having a discounting structure allows you to hold your ground, with confidence. At first, it can be a little scary to go from a negotiating environment, to a discounting-only environment. You have to trust and believe that, if they're sold on having you, and your team specifically, DJ their wedding or event, that they'll buy from you, even if you don't give a discount. Be confident. Confidence sells. Confidence, not arrogance or cockiness. They want to buy from someone who is confident in their ability to exceed their expectations. If you don't exude confidence, they'll find someone else who will, and sometimes pay them more than you, for the peace of mind. Make them want to buy from you. Help them buy from you.

Don't negotiate against yourself. If you've already given them a price for the DJ, gobo and/or lighting they want, don't give them a lower one without taking something away, or getting something else of value back (a larger deposit, reduced services, higher guest guarantee, etc.). If you give them a lower price, after you've already given them a price, you're devaluing your services. You're also negotiating against yourself, because you're the only one giving. If they ask, *"Can you do better on the price?",* you can say *"Thanks for asking, but for that date and package, that is the best price. Shall we reserve your date now?"* Make sure you're smiling when you say it, even if you're on the phone. People can tell when you're smiling when talking to them on the phone. Smiling shows that you're interested. Smiling shows that you're not offended by them asking. And, smiling shows that you're a nice person.

My favorite story about negotiating is what happened to me at an major DJ show in Las Vegas. I had a booth which featured my books, CDs and DVDs. A DJ came over and looked at one set of my DVDs that was labeled $299 (already discounted from the price on my website). He indicated that he wanted to share it with a friend, which I told him was fine. But, he walked away without buying them. A little while later, he came back holding two, new, crisp $100 bills. He was rubbing them between his fingers so I could hear the sound. He said, *"We were thinking of paying cash, and wanted to see if this would do?"* (meaning, would I take $200 instead of $299 if he paid cash). I could have been offended, after all, the set was $299 and already discounted from my website price. Instead, I looked at him, smiled, and starting looking around on the floor. I said, *"Absolutely, but I think you dropped one."* (meaning, I thought he had a third $100 bill, but had dropped it). He smiled and laughed a little. I smiled, but didn't say anything else. After a short pause he asked, *"What about another half?"* (meaning, would I take $250, instead of $299). I looked at him, and with a big smile I said *"You'd be a lot closer, wouldn't you?"* He smiled and laughed, and I smiled and laughed, but didn't say another word. He then pulled the other $100 bill out of his pocket, which was just as crisp and fresh as the other two, handed them over to me, and I gave him his DVDs. It could have gone totally differently if my initial reaction to his asking was to be offended, and to say, *"No, I won't take $200, it's $299 and already discounted from my site!"* That would have changed the whole tone of the discussion. Since I was smiling the whole time, and since I knew he was an interested buyer, I kept it moving forward. At any point, he could have walked away, without buying. The fact that he was staying there showed me his interest.

Don't devalue what you do. When you set the prices for your DJs, photo booths and lighting, have confidence in them. Price is the number you come up with. Value is the number the customer actually pays. If you have to discount to make the sale, then the value they perceive is not equal to the price. Believe that what you're delivering is worth every penny, or more, than what you're charging - even when others are charging less. There will always be someone who will charge less for, what looks on paper to be, the same services. Any business that wants to sustain for the long term will be raising their prices at some point. When you started your business, it's very possible it was you who was charging less. If you can't show your customers why they should choose you, at your price, then you're bound to lose sales. Your goal is to fill your calendar with people you like, who highly value what you do. If you can do that, it doesn't matter if someone is charging less, let them fill their own calendar with that lower-dollar business.

Lastly, on this subject, negotiate like you don't need their business, even when you do. If they sense that you're desperate for the sale, you'll either end up giving away more than you have to, or they'll choose someone else because they're afraid you may not be around when their wedding or event date arrives. If they feel that you want their business, but that you don't need it (or that it will be easy for you to book that date for another event), you'll have an easier time holding your price. Speaking of pricing, is it better to sell your DJ services, photo booth and lighting through packages or a-la-carte pricing? Let's find out.

CHAPTER 28

What's Your Opportunity Cost?

How good are your sales skills? How good are your upsell skills (selling additional products and services to them, after the initial sale, but before their event)? I was consulting with a single-op DJ (it's just him, no other DJ's in his company, so he only does one event per day), and I queried him about his sales skills. I asked him to grade his sales skills: A, B, C, D or F. He said, *"I'm a C, at best."* I thanked him for his honesty. I asked if he felt he could fill his Saturday nights in wedding season, without much trouble, given his current marketing and website. He felt that he could. So, counter to my usually-suggested 2 or 3 package recommendation, I suggested that he only offer 1 package for a Saturday night wedding, in high season. Make an all-inclusive package, with everything he had to offer (DJ, MC, ceremony sound system, uplighting, monogram projection, photo booth, dancing in the clouds, etc.). Take all of those services and add them up, then apply a reasonable discount. I explained to him that any of those items that were sitting on his warehouse shelf, on a Saturday night, were costing him money. Since he can only do one wedding on a Saturday night, he needed to maximize that revenue.

If your company can only do only one wedding or event at a time, and it's a popular in-season date, rather than trying to sell a-la-carte, or even from 3 packages (see Chapter 30), you, too could be selling a choice of 2: Do you want to have your me for your wedding/event, or not? Your sales presentation would include saying things like, *"I want choosing me for your entertainment to be the easiest decision you'll make for your wedding. I don't want you to have to worry about asking for a feature that others charge extra for, and not choosing it because of the cost. You have only one decision to make, and that's whether you want me to be the one to ensure that we take your vision and bring it to life, and that you and your guests are wowed at every turn, both with the way the music flows, from your ceremony to the dancing, as well as the creative lighting. Once you make that decision, you get all of us, and our entire bag of tricks, for one, all-inclusive price. If you want them, we'll set up as many uplights as necessary to enhance your décor. If you want the walls bathed with beautiful colors and textures, you got it. If you want a fun photo booth, I'll make it happen. So, should we reserve your date and get on to the fun parts of planning your music, timeline and décor?"*

I've mentioned "opportunity cost" a few times already, but I want to delve a little deeper so you can understand just how much money is at stake. By definition, opportunity cost is the loss of a potential gain, when another alternative is chosen. In plain language it's the profit you didn't make, because they chose a lower option. To illustrate this, I want to go back to a very smart company, McDonald's. Whether you eat there, or not, we can all agree that they're pretty good at marketing, but are they good at selling? I know many people who get upset when they place their order at McDonald's and the clerk asks *"Would you like 2 apple pies for a dollar?"* (when you didn't order any apple pies). By asking that question they've crossed over from being an order-taker, to a salesperson. If all they do is take your order, take your money and fulfill your order, they're only going to ever get the dollar value of your order. However, if they ask you if you want 2 apple pies for a dollar, or hash brown potatoes at breakfast, or an ice cream cone in the evening, they might get that additional sale… but, only if they ask you. The opportunity cost of not asking the question is the potential gain.

Some years ago I had the fortune of sitting on plane next to a Vice President from McDonald's. I asked him how often people said yes when they asked if they want 2 apple pies for a dollar. He wouldn't tell me, so I suggested that it was 1/3 of the time. He said that I was close. Working with that estimate, I mentioned to him that I lived in a small town, with only one McDonald's, and he was familiar with that particular restaurant. I guessed that they might see 500 or 600 customers a day, and he said it was more like 1,500, which surprised me.

If their cash registers ring 1,500 times each day, and if they asked everyone for the upsell (apples pies, hash browns, fries, ice cream cones, etc.) and 1/3 of the time those people said yes, that would yield them $500 additional per day. That $500 per day, every day of the year, totals $182,500 per year - if, and it's a big if - they ask the question. The opportunity cost of not asking the question is that same $182,500.

What is it costing your DJ, photo booth or lighting business to not ask for the sale for products and services they didn't originally buy, whether at the initial sale, or later during planning meetings and calls (upsells)? I also contend that after they make the initial purchase with you, and with other wedding and event pros, it's likely that their budget has already been exceeded (a WeddingWire survey showed couples exceed their wedding budgets by an average of 40%!). They may now think differently about those other items. They often look at it as a different budget. Sometimes they might even get someone else to pay for that enhancement. The important message here is that you won't get these additional sales, unless you ask for them. Can you make it a part of the planning process? Many of you have multiple contacts with the couple/customer during the planning, but before the event. Remember that I don't want you selling them things they don't want, or need. But I also don't want you not mentioning additional services just because they were on a tight budget. Let them decide. Don't make the decision for them by not asking. Maybe having better pricing and packages can help you to sell more, too. Let's see how.

CHAPTER 29

Packages vs. A-La-Carte

Wedding and event DJs and MCs are service businesses. Even though photo booths and lighting are a physical products, they're also service businesses. That may be why a lot of you don't use packages for selling. However, a lot has been written about how using packages makes it easier for you to sell, and easier for them to buy. A WeddingWire survey showed that couples prefer packages as a starting point. Your packages don't have to be exact, to the last detail. They can be a foundation, and then you can customize for them from there. Remember that I said earlier that decision fatigue is your enemy? You don't want them to have to make too many decisions before they buy. Let them make the decision on which songs, which color lighting, which gobo design they want, after they buy. When you go out to dinner, which do you choose first, the restaurant or what you're going to eat? Get the sale. Take them out of the market, and out of the mindset of a buyer, and into the mindset of a customer.

Value meals at McDonald's, and other fast food chains, show how they use packages to increase their average sale. By offering a discount for buying the multiple items (sandwich, drink and fries), it encourages consumers to spend more. The opportunity cost of not having the package is the difference between what they could buy (the higher-dollar value meal) versus what they might have bought (which would be less drinks, and less fries). McDonald's sells and delivers at the same time. In your case, you have more time before their event to upsell them. There's still an opportunity cost, but you have weeks, or months, to reduce that, by upselling them to services and products they didn't originally buy.

This isn't just for fast food, or low-priced items. Most, if not all car manufacturers, including Mercedes Benz, Audi and BMW, have packages which are discounted from the a-la-carte pricing for those features. In some cases, you can't get some of the items without buying the package. You can try that as well. Put together a group of popular products or services, and give the package an aspirational name (The Crystal Package, The Millennium Package, etc., as opposed to Package A, B, C). Don't just list the items in the package, editorialize the items to show them how they will help them. You're selling "why" they should choose your entertainment company, not "what" you do. Anyone can do "what" you do. We want them to specifically want you for their wedding or event DJ and have their lighting specifically from you, and that's in the "why" (see Chapter 13).

For example, if you're selling uplighting as a décor option, write, *"Uplighting– enhance the design experience for you and your guests by having the colors from your theme extend beyond the linens and flowers, to bathe the walls in your choice of hues."*

How much money are you leaving on the table by selling your DJ, photo booth and lighting services a-la-carte? In other words, what's the opportunity cost of them not buying additional products and services that would enhance their wedding or event? I don't want you to sell them things they don't need, just so you can make more money. I'm talking about the things that you know would make their event better, but they either choose not to have them, or they didn't even know they could have. One of the things that packages do well is to showcase those additional products and services, and legitimize them as choices. I've heard time and time again, from businesses just like yours, that grouping products or services has helped them sell more.

A few years ago a wedding DJ came up to me at a conference and gave me a big hug, and said, *"Thank you!"*, to which I replied, *"What did I do to deserve this hug?"* She explained that the previous year, at the same conference, I had suggested that she have 3 packages:

1) **A low package,** which she'd be willing to do, but maybe with restrictions (not on a Saturday in high-season, etc.).

2) **The middle package,** which she wants to, and expects to sell the most of. This should have good profit, as you'll end up selling more of these because it's in the middle (see the next chapter).

3) **An aspirational top package** – put everything in as an all-inclusive, everything including the kitchen sink, top package.

After creating the entertainment/lighting packages, and having them professionally designed and printed, the first couple to come in and see them bought the top package for their wedding. She told me that I deserved the thanks, and the hug, because in 8 years in business, they had never sold anything that expensive. It was their highest sale to date. I explained that having the packages created, designed and printed, legitimized the choices. The customer that bought the top package had prioritized their service, and had valued having her company provide those services. Some people want the best of what you offer. However, if you give them those items one at a time, decision fatigue starts to set in, and with so many decisions to make, you often end up at a lower price point, than if you had a package with those services.

Imagine walking into a restaurant, and instead of getting a menu, you're handed a list of ingredients in the kitchen. Does that make it easier, or harder to order your dinner? Of course it makes it harder. Most people, other than chefs, wouldn't know where to start. The menu is simply a package of ingredients, prepared in a preset way, and presented to you in a predetermined manner. That works whether your entrée is $10 or $150. Take that up one level and consider the 3-course, Prix-Fixe Menu, where you get to choose one appetizer, one entrée and one dessert for a fixed price. Your choice is easier because price is no longer a factor. Any of the choices will cost the same, and any supplements (up-charges for specific items) are clearly labeled. At The French Laundry, a very high end restaurant in the wine country of Northern California, they only serve the "chef's tasting menu," which changes every day. You can choose anything on the menu for one set price, currently $350 to $450 per person, including service charge, but not including your drinks or tax. If you choose all of the supplemental items it can go over $600 for one person, plus drinks! I think we can all agree that this is a high-end establishment. Yet, the concept of a package, in this case a prix-fixe menu, works. They have a waiting list for reservations, and you're recommended to make your reservation 6 months, or more, in advance... and you pay when you make your reservation! The people that can afford to dine there want it even more, because of the scarcity (see "Veblen Goods" in Chapter 31).

My simple mantra when it comes to sales is, *"Make it easy for you to sell, and easy for them to buy."* Using packages makes it easier for you to sell your services, and easier for your customers to buy them. You can still customize their services, products and experience, you just start from a different place. It's like creating a website for your DJ, photo booth or lighting business, from scratch versus using a template. A template that allows customization is a better starting point because it's easier to focus on what you want to change. If the template has little, or no customization, you'd probably pass and find another one. Similarly, if your packages are "take-it-or-leave-it", your customers might decide to pass as well. By taking your a-la-carte services, and making packages, you create a better starting point. If you're selling a gobo (monogram projection), do you really need to know which style they want before you write the contract? Or, is it enough to know that they have a choice of styles, from a preset list, and they can make those choices later?

I did sales consulting for a caterer who wouldn't write a contract for a wedding or event until he had laid out the entire menu proposal for the client. There are two problems with that structure: 1) you delay getting them to commit to you and 2) you end up doing a lot of detailed proposal writing, and menu creation, without guarantee of the sale. I told him there are caterers all over the country, and all over the world, who are writing contracts for weddings and events, without having the exact menu items. As I mentioned earlier, when you go out to eat, you first choose the restaurant, then you choose what you're going to eat. Help them choose you as the DJ, and then create their "menu". I'm often contracted to speak at events without knowing exactly which of my topics I'll be presenting. I know how many topics, and for how long, but not specifically which ones. I don't need to know which ones... yet. I will know well before the event, as they need to create the marketing materials, website, ticketing, etc. My list of topics is extensive, but still limited, very much like your choices. Your customers have to make one important decision first, before needing the details, and that's whether they want you to be their wedding or event DJ, and whether they want you, and only you (and your team) to do the lighting and/or photo booth for their wedding or event. The rest of the details are secondary. They can't get your results, until they decide they want to get them from you. Don't complicate it for them.

Some of you are thinking, *"But Alan, everything I do is custom! I can't do packages and I can't quote them on the spot."* I understand that each wedding, bar/bat mitzvah, quinceañera, prom and corporate event is unique. But if you've been doing this for a while, you can look back and see the patterns of products/services that are most popular with your customers. You can create packages that include certain items and have them decide on the actual items later. Remember, your mission is to get them to commit to choosing your company first, then get into the details, later. Other companies can buy that same equipment, often from the same suppliers, so you rarely (if ever) have a monopoly on the brands you use. You do, however, have a monopoly if they want you and your team, to take that equipment and create a unique experience for their wedding or event.

When I'm consulting with an entertainment company who thinks that they can't do packages, we take a look at the weddings and events that they've done in the past couple of years. We put them on spreadsheets, making a column for each product or service that was used for that event. What I'd be trying to do is itemize the components of those events. Then, we can analyze and look for patterns and combinations of similar products and services. Most of the time natural patterns emerge. Those patterns were created by you, and your past clients, but were influenced by your personal style and creativity. While the look and feel of the individual lighting and special-effects items was surely different, from a higher level there are almost always natural patterns which allow you to create packages that are starting points. You can customize for them once they've chosen a starting point. It's like getting a head start, instead of starting from a blank sheet. How many packages should you have? Let's find out.

CHAPTER 30

The Power of 3's

I mentioned that having 3 packages is best, but some of you are wondering why, or thinking that you have too many options to only have 3 packages. First, let me clarify that your entertainment company can have as many packages as you'd like. However, I recommend only showing up to 3 options to any one customer. No one needs to know everything that you do, it leads to indecision. After you've discussed the basic needs of the customer you'll know which of your packages will, and will not, fulfill their needs. Then you can present them with only the packages that will work for them. This applies not just to packages, but to everything you sell. If you're selling lighting, you know that bringing them too many choices only leads to confusion. When a particular lighting option isn't a good fit for their theme, take it out of sight. You don't want them seeing it any longer, as it's only going to confuse them. Ideally you want to get them down to 2 choices, so you can apply the "choice close" and ask if they want choice A or B. If you're selling gobos, there are surely many style and color options. First, find out more details about what they need, and then pitch them only the options that will work for those needs.

If you've ever seen the TV show *"House Hunters"*, they first narrow the house buyers to 3 houses from which to choose (without showing us all of the other houses they had seen). Then, in the second-to-last scene of the show, they make them eliminate one choice, so they're down to only 2 houses. That's an important step, because it's harder to decide from an array of 3 than from 2. Once they're down to the last 2 houses, they apply the choice-close and ask them which one they want to buy. Similarly, it's your job to start them with more choices, but as quickly as you can, eliminate some choices, until the right one, or two, become obvious. When someone is trying to decide which of my speaking topics to have me present at their event, I first ask them to tell me about the audience, and any other speakers at this, or prior events. Have I presented in their city before? Has their audience heard me present live, or on webinars? As we're talking, I'm eliminating certain topics. Then, I can suggest just the right program for them, or at least narrow their choices from my many topics, down to a short list.

So, why does 3 work? There are a lot of situations where the "rule of 3's" applies. Comedians use 3's when leading up to a punchline. The TV show *"Let's Make a Deal"* has

3 doors, because more would take too long. I did a search online and found this on Psychotactics.com, *"The brain finds it relatively easy to grasp threes — elements, colours and fonts. Push that marginally up to four and the brain gets confused about where to look and what to do, and sends the eye scampering like a frisky puppy on a sunny day."*

People also perceive the item in the middle to be the best choice. That's why I said earlier to create your 3 packages and have the one in the middle be the one you expect to sell the most. There's actual science behind this. According to the Journal of Consumer Psychology it's called the **"Center-Stage Effect"**. They explain that *"consumers believe that options placed in the center of a simultaneously presented array are the most popular."* As a matter of fact, if you label the middle package your *"most popular"*, it's likely to become your most popular. There's safety in numbers here. People perceive that most people buy the middle package, therefore it's a safe choice for them, too.

When the hamburger chain Wendy's first started they only had one size of hamburger. It wasn't called a "single" back then, because that's all they had. Their point of differentiation was that it was bigger and square. Later, when they came out with a double hamburger, they didn't sell well - at all. Their marketing consultant suggested that they come out with a triple hamburger. They were perplexed as to why they would make a triple hamburger, when no one was buying the doubles, but they tried it. When the triple came out, double hamburgers started selling. When the double was the highest choice, it wasn't as desirable, but when it became the middle choice, it was a safer decision. You didn't feel like you were splurging when the double was the middle option, as you were when it was the biggest choice. That said, some people will opt for your top package, or choice, as they want only the best that you have to offer. If entertainment and lighting is high on their priorities list, you just might sell more to them by having packages. If you start to sell from the top-down, you'll make even more from each wedding or event. Let's see how.

CHAPTER 31

Top Down Selling for a Better Bottom Line

It's your job to be their expert and guide. Let them decide whether to add a photo booth and lighting services, or not, regardless of their budget. That's called Top Down Selling. It's much easier to start from a higher price point and work down, than it is to sell them at a lower point and get them to add more. In an article called *"Top Down Selling Can Generate Higher Average Sales"* the author, Doug Holman, says *"Consumers rarely make a buying decision at a low price point and then decide to spend more money when additional information is provided."* In other words, it's easier if you just sell them more up front, rather than selling a low package and trying to get them to buy more later, especially if you're not good at upselling. This is where having better entertainment, photo booth and lighting packages can help you. As with the story I told earlier, having the aspirational package helped that wedding DJ sell more services, for higher dollars, than she had ever done before.

Consumers also expect to pay the first number they see. That's why I advocate using a price range, as my favorite of the 4 ways to handle pricing inquiries (from Chapter 12). That way they don't hear, or see, just one number. They see the range (framing the price for them). If you include your most popular price point, or range, within that larger range, you're dealing with a level of transparency that can foster trust. They don't feel as if you're being evasive. Just the opposite, your transparency can help make others look to be opaque and evasive.

Top down selling is about raising your average sale, so that you can make more profit from doing the same number of weddings and events. You get more bang for your customers' bucks, and so do they, in the form of additional products and services. When you learn how to raise your average sale, as your volume goes up, you get an exponential effect of even more profits.

There are 3 ways for you to make more money:
1) **Volume** - Do more weddings and events
2) **Have a higher average sale** – through higher prices, and/or selling more to each customer
3) **Both of the above**

The problem with more volume is that many of you are maxed-out, and can't, or don't want to do more weddings or events. Whether it's a physical inventory problem (you don't have enough photo booths2), or a talent problem (you can't do two weddings/events at a time if you only have one

DJ), a personnel problem (you don't have enough support people to handle more weddings/events), or just a short-on-time problem (which we all run into at some point) – there just isn't any more time left to handle more customers. Once you run out of inventory, you can't do more weddings and events. Now, if there's strong demand for your services, and you're running out of inventory, you may have pricing power, and you can, and should test raising your rates. If you can still fill your calendar at the higher rates, then you're making more profit from the same number of events.

Can you raise your DJ, lighting and photo booth rental rates now? If you had charged each customer $50 more last year (total, not per person), how many would have said "No"? If some would have said *"No"*, would the increase in dollars from the others make up for the ones you would have lost? Could you have booked others to fill those dates who would have paid $50 more? You have pricing power when enough people are still saying yes to fill your calendar. You may get more noes at the higher price, but if you're still filling your calendar, that's OK. As I've raised my prices I certainly hear more noes. But I also get lots of yeses. I've actually found that now, at the highest rates I've ever had, I get less price resistance. People expect it to be higher, and when they hear the number, it only makes them want to find a way to make it happen even more. Try running this price exercise at different increases. What would happen with a $50 increase, or $100 increase, or $500 increase, or more? What about 5% or 10% increases? Find the "sweet spot" where you can still fill your calendar. It's OK that you get people saying "no", as long as you get enough saying "yes".

Some people don't think it's high enough quality if they don't pay a lot. In economics there are things called "Veblen Goods", named for American economist and sociologist, Thorstein Veblen. Wikipedia says *"Veblen goods are types of luxury goods, such as expensive wines, jewelry, fashion-designer handbags, and luxury cars, which are in demand because of the high prices asked for them. The high price makes the goods desirable as symbols of the buyer's high social status."* In other words, they're more desirable because of the high price and low supply. They actually become less desirable as the price comes down and availability gets higher. When more people can afford, and get these goods, the status-seekers don't want them. If yours is a luxury DJ or entertainment brand, or you're going after the luxury consumer, you may have to have a high price, just to get their attention and respect. If the price is too low, they may not want it. A DJ friend/client of mine was hired and flown across the country, because the client wanted *"The most expensive MC in New York!"*

Whether you can raise your rates, or not (and most of you

can raise your rates, at least a little, you're just afraid to try it), increasing your average sale is something that almost everyone can do. Unless you only sell one thing, at one fixed price, you probably have products and/or services that some clients don't buy, even though they would make their wedding or event, better. Using packages to sell more, up front, is one way. Being sure to bring up other lighting, photo booth or design/décor options, every time you speak with them, is another. If, when discussing some detail of their wedding or event, you feel that some other product or service, would be right for them, you should tell them. If they ask how much more it will cost, tell them, and don't apologize for it. Don't say things like, *"Sorry, that will cost extra."* Instead use a confident voice or writing style, and say *"For all of that it's only $X. Should I add that to your order?"* If they want it, they can say "yes".

If they pose an objection, welcome it. That means that they want it, they just aren't ready to commit, yet. If they say that they're already paying a lot to you, go back to the chapters on objections (Chapters 23-24), hold your ground and use feel-felt-found (even if you don't always use those words), *"I understand how you feel, and I know how things seem to add up for your wedding. I was having a similar conversation with another couple last week, and they realized that this was more real, than reality TV. There's no do-over. There's *no second chance to get it right, and they wanted it to be just right. So they, too, added a few more things, just like you, to ensure it was everything they were imagining. Shall I get that added to your order?"* (and smile while you say it).

There's a TV show called *"Property Brothers"*, that features twin brothers. One is a real estate agent and the other is a contractor. Home buyers come to them and give them a wish list of their ideal home: the neighborhood, the number of bedrooms and baths, the size, the amenities, the school district - everything they want, including their budget. The brothers go about finding them a home, and then bring the home buyers in to see the house. The house appears to have everything they want, and more. They leave the home buyer to tour the house, and the more they do, they more they love it. Then they ask them how much they think the house costs, and the home buyer always guesses a number a little above their budget. In reality, the price is always way above their budget, sometimes even double the amount. The home buyer is upset that the brothers would show them a house that's so expensive. But, they explain that to get everything they want, in that neighborhood, will cost that higher amount. The home buyer is left to decide whether to raise their budget, or to compromise for a different house, either in a different area, without some of the things on their wish list, or both. This is an example of top down selling.

They don't apologize for showing them the more expensive house. After all, it has everything they want, and more. They're just showing them what they've asked for. You should do the same thing. Ask good questions, find out what they want, find out their budget, and show them a package of products and services that meets their needs, and wants, regardless of their budget. Let them decide if it's too much, or not.

When I was speaking in Mumbai, India, there was a gentleman from a 5-Star hotel at the event. He related a story of a father who came in for his daughter's wedding. He told them he had a 400,000 rupee budget (at the time about $5,800 US). When he showed him what they wanted, and gave the price, it was 850,000 rupees (over $12,400 US), more than double their stated budget. The father then asked if they could do that package for 800,000 rupees (double the original budget). It just shows that if a consumer can find what they want and need, at a lower price, they'll buy it. If they can't, then they either have to raise their budget, or rethink their priorities, because the money always follows the priorities. You and I do the same thing. We spend in proportion to our priorities, and we save when it's not as important. Learn to present each customer with higher packages of products and services, when warranted by their needs, and you can raise your average sale. That's the cornerstone of top down selling.

CHAPTER 32

Follow Up to increase your profits

Just as the customer isn't going to say *"sign me up"*, they're also not going to automatically follow up with you after an appointment. That's your job. Your first goal is to close the sale today. If they don't reserve your DJ services, lighting or photo booth today, your second goal is to not let them leave without getting agreement as to how, and when you're going to follow up with them. Ambiguous next steps lead to ambiguous results! You need to test how serious they are about buying from you. So, ask for a follow-up appointment. For instance, if they say that they want to think about it and get back to you, say, *"Of course you do, it's a big decision. Let's schedule a time for you to come back so we can help you make the final decision. How about the same time on Thursday?"* The key parts to this are agreeing with their objection (we want to think about it – of course you do), and using a confident statement that you feel they want to come back. If they agree to the appointment, you likely do have a sale. It's not assured, as they could still be going to see someone else, but it's a really good sign.

If they don't agree to the follow up appointment, then say,

"*No worries, I'll just call you on Thursday to see if you have any questions. Is 11 a.m. or 7 p.m. better for me to call?*" Even if they agree to the call, it doesn't mean they'll be there or that they'll answer it. But again, it's a good sign. If you're getting push-back to this as well, then just let them go and say that you'll follow up with them soon, and that they can get back to you if they have any questions.

I hear from a lot of DJs that you try to call, and call, and they never answer. From what I've read on Gen Y and Gen Z, this is common. They prefer digital communications over phone calls. If you do call, leave a message, as they might be screening their calls. Make it a short message, and have something of value to say, rather than that you're just calling to "touch base". Did they ask a question for which you had to research an answer? Did you see an article that you thought they'd enjoy reading? Always try to have something of value when you reach out, whether by phone, text, or email.

If you email, and they don't reply, make sure you asked one question at the end of your email (tip number 6 in my book *"Why Don't They Call Me?"*). Also make sure you kept it short. If they don't respond, it could be that they didn't receive your email, there was no reason for them to reply (no question at the end of your email), or they've decided to go with another entertainment company. You want to get an answer. You don't want a "maybe". Maybe is a salesperson's nightmare. It means nothing. It's not a sale, and yet they're still a possibility. You'd always rather have a "no", than a "maybe". A "no" is closure.

You can escalate your emails from "*following up*" to *"Have you made a decision on your entertainment?"* or *"If you've decided to go with someone else for your DJ, best of luck with your wedding. Please just reply and let me know so I can take you off my list. If not, would you like to discuss how we can make your day amazing, and have your guests raving about your wedding?"* I've even read about, and personally received some funny emails from companies that are trying to sell me their services. After a few attempts, I received this email:

> "*Hey,*
> *I tried to contact you regarding helping you with your online store at alanberg.com and haven't heard back from you.*
> *We help online stores like yours from just $79 per month. Let me know if:*
> *1. You're interested and want to talk.*
> *2. You're interested but just haven't responded yet.*
> *3. You're all set with your online cart, and I should stop bothering you.*
> *4. I should follow up in three months.*
> *5. You're being chased by a bear and need me to call Animal Police.*
> *Reply with a number from 1 to 5."*

If nothing else, it made me smile, and feel a little different about the person who sent it. It makes them seem real, and not like it was a computer program. Just the other day I received this one:

> "Alan, I haven't heard back from you and this tells me 1 of 3 things:
> 1. You are swimming in revenue and would not accept one more lead even if they begged you.
> 2. You already have this covered and just haven't had time to reply with "go away, Smith (his last name)".
> 3. You're playing hard to get and the fourth email is the charm.
>
> Please let me know which one it is because I'm starting to think about losing sleep. Thanks in advance and I am looking forward to hearing from you."

This also got my attention, and yes it made me smile, too. Did either of these work? Well, I did go and check out their websites to see what they do. I'm just not in the market for their services. You have an edge. Your customer has made the first move and reached out to you, showing interest and a strong buying signal. I didn't reach out to either of these companies, so they didn't get that buying signal from me, but kudos to them for trying and being persistent, and different.

I was consulting with a DJ recently and we saw that he had only been trying once to contact couples when they inquired. We emailed a bride who had reached out a month before, and using my tips he got a reply in minutes, had a call with her that night, and booked the sale. Don't give up! 💡

CHAPTER 33

You can't do their wedding or event, if you don't close the sale

How do you feel now? Are you going to close more sales? Your goal is to be able to do more weddings, social and corporate events, for the people you like, and to be paid the money you deserve. It all starts with having better questioning, listening and sales skills. After all, if you don't close the sale, you can't do their wedding/event. What I want you to do is take small pieces of what you've learned in this book and apply them, today. Whether it's in how you answer the next price inquiry, or how you navigate your next phone, in-person or virtual appointment, small changes can have a big effect.

Asking better questions is simply about focusing on your customers, and helping them buy. Guide them to share with you what's important to them, and the outcome of their wedding or event. Don't over think it. There's no magic script that will work for everyone. You need to find your own voice, because it's one of the only things on which you have a monopoly. Your competition can copy almost everything you do, but they can never be you.

This is not going to happen overnight. Don't strive for perfection, just strive to be better, every day, with every customer. Besides improving your craft skills (mixing, MC'ing, production, décor, etc.), you can also learn to be a better listener. You can be better at having a real, meaningful conversation via email, Facebook Messenger, Zoom, Skype, WhatsApp or text. You can be better at closing the sale, when it's ready to be closed, as opposed to some specific time in your pitch (which you're going to ditch, anyway).

So, what are you going to do differently today, even if it makes you feel just a little uncomfortable? It's a lot less scary once you've tried it, and it works for you. Trust the scores of wedding and event DJs who are already shutting up and selling more. Thank you for taking the time to read this book. Please share your stories of success with me at **SellMore@AlanBerg.com**

FROM THE AUTHOR

Who is Alan Berg? If I had to answer this in one sentence, I'd say "I'm a Suburban Renaissance Man". I'm a husband, father, son, brother, friend, speaker, author, salesman, marketer, musician, handyman, consultant, teacher and, I've been told, an all-around nice guy. I'm passionate about my family and my work. I love being creative and working with my hands as well as my mind. That's one of the reasons there's a wrench in my personal logo.

I've worked in sales, marketing and sales management for over 25 years, over 20 in wedding business media. I spent 11 years at The Knot (at the time the largest, busiest wedding media site in the world), most as Vice President of Sales and Vice President of The Knot Market Intelligence. I'm a professional speaker and proud member of the National Speakers Association, the leading organization for professional speakers, where I've been honored to earn my Certified Speaking Professional® (CSP), the highest earned designation for a professional member - which makes me one of only about 800 in the world. I'm also been privileged to be, as of this writing, one of only 36 Global Speaking Fellows in the world (through the Global Speakers Federation).

I revel in the success of others and truly believe that your success will lead to more success for me and for everyone.

I believe that when you give first, you'll get more than you could have ever asked for in return. I also believe in living for today, while planning for tomorrow. I know that this information can help you, as it has for so many others, and I appreciate you picking up my book. I look forward to hearing how you've implemented these ideas.

Thank you.

Please post your thoughts about this book on Amazon at: www.ReviewMyBooks.net

In addition to writing books and articles I have the privilege of traveling around the country, and internationally, performing keynote addresses and workshops in 14 countries, as well as doing in-house sales trainings. If you'd like to have me speak for your company, conference, group or association, train your sales and customer support teams, have me review your website or help you with consulting services (virtual or in-person), please contact me directly:

- email: **Alan@AlanBerg.com**
- visit: **www.AlanBerg.com**
- call/text: **732.422.6362**
- international: **+1 732 422 6362**
- WhatsApp: **+1.732.289.4842**

ABOUT THE AUTHOR

Alan Berg is fluent in the language of business. He's been in marketing, sales and sales management for over 20 years, working with entertainment businesses, like yours, in the wedding and events industry. Before striking out on his own as a business consultant, author and professional speaker, he served as Vice President of Sales and The Knot Market Intelligence at The Knot (now The Knot Worldwide), at the time the leading life stage media company. In additional to his speaking and consulting he also serves as a consultant and Educator for WeddingPro (the education arm of WeddingWire and The Knot), doing webinars, live presentations, writing articles and more. Alan is the wedding & event industry's only Certified Speaking Professional®, the highest earned designation for a professional member of the National Speakers Association. And, as of this writing, he's one of only 36 Global Speaking Fellows in the world.

He's able to help new businesses and solopreneurs, as well as established players and corporations, understand and achieve their goals. Alan understands business as he's owned several of his own, including publishing two wedding magazines. He understands what it's like to make payroll, do the books, do collections, apply for a loan and manage/hire/fire/train employees. He knows what you're going through, feels your pain and can help ease it. Increasing sales and profitability are wonderful remedies!

Through his extensive experience, speaking and consulting domestically and internationally (14 countries, on 5 continents, 5 of them presenting in Spanish, and counting), Alan understands that the needs of entertainment businesses are not that different from the needs of all businesses. You all want to find, capture and retain customers. If you're reading this book you want actionable content, not exhaustive homework and that's what you'll get. Get started now on your journey to greater success.

Share Alan's unique inspirational, actionable content

If you'd like to have Alan speak for your company, conference, group or association, to thank your key partners for their referrals, for bulk copies of this book to inspire your team or members - including custom editions with your branding, and to find out about his website review and consulting services for your business, large or small (yes, even if you're the only employee), contact Alan directly:

- email: **Alan@AlanBerg.com**
- visit: **www.AlanBerg.com**
- call/text: **732.422.6362**
- international: **+1 732 422 6362**
- WhatsApp: **+1.732.289.4842**

Have Alan teach these techniques to your team or group:

If you'd like to have Alan do on-site, or remote/virtual Private Sales Training, or a small group Mastermind Day to teach these techniques, and more, whether you're a team of 1, 5 or 50, contact Alan directly:

- email: **Alan@AlanBerg.com**
- visit: **www.AlanBerg.com**
- call/text: **+1.732.422.6362**
- international: **+1 732 422 6362**

"I cannot believe I waited this long for an actual training with Alan. His knowledge and delivery is second to none. If you want to grow your business and want to truly work on your sales strategy, Alan is an integral part of that process."
Heather Laughman, HD Entertainment, Gettysburg, PA

"I enjoyed the things he taught me and have already had some success just applying the principal of using my ears more than my mouth. You are good at what you do and you make people better at what they do."
Steve McDowell, Fantasy Sound, Livermore, CA

"You seriously need to Shut Up and Listen to Alan Berg!!! Being a down to earth person to talk to he is a wonderful speaker. I have learned to so much from him. My business is growing and all I did was LISTEN."
Sarah Martin, Shutterbooth, Detroit, MI

www.ingramcontent.com/pod-product-compliance
Lightning Source LLC
Chambersburg PA
CBHW052022290426
44112CB00014B/2340